Palgrave Studies in Race, Ethnicity, Indigeneity and Criminal Justice

This pioneering series brings much-needed attention to minority, excluded, and marginalised perspectives in criminology, centred on the topic of 'race' and the racialization of crime and criminal justice systems. It draws on a range of theoretical approaches including critical race theory, critical criminology, postcolonial theory, intersectional approaches and Indigenous theory. The series seeks to challenge and broaden the current discourse, debates and discussions within contemporary criminology as a whole, including drawing on the voices of Indigenous people and those from the Global South which are often silenced in favour of dominant white discourses in Criminology.

More information about this series at
https://link.springer.com/bookseries/15777

Nicole Watson

Aboriginal Women, Law and Critical Race Theory

Storytelling From The Margins

palgrave
macmillan

Nicole Watson
Nura Gili Centre for Indigenous
Programs
University of New South Wales
Sydney, NSW, Australia

Palgrave Studies in Race, Ethnicity, Indigeneity and Criminal Justice
ISBN 978-3-030-87326-4 ISBN 978-3-030-87327-1 (eBook)
https://doi.org/10.1007/978-3-030-87327-1

This Palgrave Macmillan imprint is published by the registered company Springer Nature Switzerland AG
The registered company address is: Gewerbestrasse 11, 6330 Cham, Switzerland

This book is dedicated to the matriarchs in my life, who have provided me with love, encouragement and humour.

Acknowledgements

I would like to express my gratitude for the support of the Australian Research Council ('ARC').[1] I thank my colleague, Professor Heather Douglas for her feedback on my draft chapters. I would also like to acknowledge Kathy Frankland of Community and Personal Histories, Queensland Department of Aboriginal and Torres Strait Islander Partnerships, for her assistance in reimagining the life of Eliza Woree in Chapter 4. Finally, I thank my husband, Russell, for his love and support.

[1] Together with Professor Heather Douglas, I was a recipient of a Discovery (Indigenous) grant and a Discovery Australian Aboriginal and Torres Strait Islander Award ('Bringing Indigenous Voices into Judicial Decision Making' IN18000021).

Contents

About the Author

Nicole Watson is a member of the Birri Gubba People who hail from Central Queensland and the Munanjali of Beaudesert, Queensland. Nicole is a legal scholar, a former columnist with the *National Indigenous Times*, and she has also published a crime novel. Nicole is the Director of the Academic Unit of the Nura Gili Centre for Indigenous Programs, University of New South Wales.

CHAPTER 1

Introduction

Abstract This chapter begins by acknowledging the nexus between the research that evolved into the pages of this book and the author's own story. That story springs from a childhood that was immersed in vibrant oral histories, and influenced by wise and powerful Black matriarchs. It is because of her own story that the writer was drawn to critical race theory; a revolutionary movement that challenges the prevailing racial hierarchy with the stories of those who live on the margins. This chapter moves on to provide a summary of the content of the remaining chapters.

Keywords Introduction · Indigenous women · Law

Introduction

Storytelling is fundamental to Indigenous cultures. It is through stories that one generation teaches the next how to care for the Country that sustains us. Within our stories are the journeys of the ancestral beings that shaped the lands and waters, and left laws that govern relationships between all living things. Stories are also sources of theory and methods

N. Watson, *Aboriginal Women, Law and Critical Race Theory*, Palgrave Studies in Race, Ethnicity, Indigeneity and Criminal Justice, https://doi.org/10.1007/978-3-030-87327-1_1

of research.[1] One of the precepts of Indigenous research methodologies is that knowledge is situated. The researcher's culture, life trajectory and ways of seeing the world all have an impact on the development of the story that becomes research.[2] The nexus between self and story is understood by scholars who write themselves into their work, and thereby render themselves accountable for their own biases.[3] The act of sharing stories also makes us vulnerable, and therefore, conscious of the need to treat the stories of others with sensitivity and respect.[4] It is with these truths in mind that I will share my own story.

As an Aboriginal person from Queensland, I call myself a 'Murri'. From my paternal grandfather, I inherited my connection to the Birri Gubba of the Bowen Basin. My paternal grandmother belonged to the Munanjali of Beaudesert. But long before I came into this world, they had created a life for themselves and their six children in the state's capital, Brisbane. It was in Brisbane that their eldest son, Sam Watson would meet the love of his life, Catherine de Gunst. They would go on to have two children, Samuel Wagan and me.

The adults of our childhood were master storytellers. It was through their words and gestures that my brother and I were introduced to the stories of cherished grandparents, aunts and uncles. Our Elders survived family separations, removal from their Country and the callous indifference of those within Queensland's Indigenous affairs bureaucracy. Even though some of the violence that they suffered continued to be inflicted upon their children, our Elders never lost hope.

It was through stories that my brother and I came to revere strong Black women such as my paternal grandmother, who we called 'Nanna'. One of the stories that Nanna shared with us concerned her certificate of exemption. The certificate provided relief from the provisions of the

[1] Margaret Kovach, *Indigenous Methodologies: Characteristics, Conversations and Contexts* (University of Toronto Press, 2009).

[2] Elizabeth Fast and Margaret Kovach, 'Community Relationships Within Indigenous Methodologies' in Sweeney Windchief and Timothy San Pedro (eds), *Applying Indigenous Research Methods: Storying with Peoples and Communities* (Routledge, 2019), 21, 25.

[3] Ibid.

[4] Ibid., 26.

dreaded protectionist legislation.[5] Those subject to the legislation were vulnerable to removal to one of Queensland's Reserves, where life was characterised by oppressive regulation, neglect and starvation. The certificate of exemption may have offered Nanna a path to relative freedom, but it almost certainly demanded a high price. Only those who could demonstrate an ability to assimilate were granted the invidious piece of paper.

I never did cast my eyes on her certificate of exemption, but I understand that Nanna held onto it throughout her life. Later, when I went to university, I met other Aboriginal students whose parents and grandparents had also been issued certificates of exemption. I was surprised to discover that, like Nanna, they too had kept those infamous pieces of paper. Some retained the certificates as proof of the indignities they had endured. But others had been so wounded by their experiences that they still expected to be woken in the middle of the night, to find a protector[6] lurking in the doorway.

Like the other matriarchs in our community, Nanna was resilient. Poverty was never far from her young family, but Nanna kept them together. My father would often reminisce about having to accompany his mother early in the mornings, as they dug for the worms that they would sell for bait. It was a chore that he loathed, but one that helped to put food on the table. After her children left home, Nanna rose through the ranks of the Commonwealth Public Service. She served on the boards of community organisations and cared for her growing number of grandchildren.

More so than anyone else, it was Nanna who encouraged me to go to Law School, where I was introduced to legal storytelling. Although the writing style of some judges was unnecessarily verbose, I was intrigued by the precision with which others framed the questions to be determined and the clarity that they brought to complex, and at times conflicting principles of law. However, women like Nanna never emerged in legal storytelling. On the rare occasions that Black women featured in the judgments that we studied, their stories were missing.

[5] The first such Act passed in Queensland was the *Aboriginals Protection and Restriction of the Sale of Opium Act 1897* (Qld). It would be repealed and replaced by the *Aboriginals Preservation and Protection Act 1939* (Qld).

[6] Protectors, who were invariably police officers, were responsible for the supervision of Indigenous wards, and oversaw matters such as the brokering of employment agreements.

It was not until many years later, as a junior scholar, that I was empowered to challenge the absence of Aboriginal women's stories from judgments through my exposure to critical race theory ('CRT'). This revolutionary movement was founded by legal scholars in the closing decades of the twentieth century to develop new methods of challenging America's racial hierarchy. One of the tenets of CRT is that racism is omnipresent.[7] It resounds in overt acts, subtle gestures and institutional practices. Because racism is so entrenched in American society it has become normal,[8] and those who sit at the apex of the hierarchy are often oblivious to their privileges. One of the tools championed by CRT scholars is storytelling. Through engaging with the narratives of outsiders, CRT scholars give voice to those who have been dehumanised by laws that are ostensibly neutral, and challenge the prevailing narrative that racism has become an aberration.[9]

This book draws upon storytelling and a paper written by the scholar, Monica J. Evans, on Black women and outlaw culture.[10] Evans argues that African American women are the pioneers of an outlaw culture that consists of empowering practices that have been created in response to the ongoing denial of the law's protection. Among the champions of outlaw culture are individuals who broke the law, such as Harriet Tubman. On occasion, however, outlaw culture has also included practices of strict adherence to law. By way of example, the Black Clubwomen of the early twentieth century operated within the confines of law and focused on uplifting their communities through social welfare programs. The Clubwomen recognised that many Black mothers were compelled, by necessity, to work outside of the home. Consequently, they established kindergartens, schools and day nurseries.[11]

[7] André Douglas Pond Cummings, 'A Furious Kinship: Critical Race Theory and the Hip-Hop Nation' in Richard Delgado and Jean Stefancic (eds), *Critical Race Theory: The Cutting Edge* (Temple University Press, 3rd ed, 2013), 107, 108.

[8] Ibid.

[9] Richard Delgado, 'Storytelling for Oppositionists and Others: A Plea for Narrative' in Richard Delgado and Jean Stefancic (eds), *Critical Race Theory: The Cutting Edge* (Temple University Press, 3rd ed, 2013), 71.

[10] Monica J. Evans, 'Stealing Away: Black Women, Outlaw Culture and the Rhetoric of Rights' (1993) 28(2) *Harvard Civil Rights—Civil Liberties Law Review*, 263.

[11] Eileen Boris, 'The Power of Motherhood: Black and White Activist Women Redefine the "Political"' (1989) 2(1) *Yale Journal of Law and Feminism*, 25, 41.

It is the central premise of this book that generations of Indigenous women in Australia have similarly been at the helm of an outlaw culture, which consists of tactics, values and strategies that operate both within and outside of the law. Due to their invisibility, Indigenous women proponents of outlaw culture have been largely overlooked by scholars. This book will use the medium of storytelling to cast light on the narratives of those who have been at the cutting edge of this body of empowering practices.

Before discussing the chapters of this book, it is necessary to clarify two issues. The first concerns the use of language. In Australia there is a multiplicity of views regarding the appropriateness of terms such as 'Aboriginal and Torres Strait Islander', 'Indigenous' and 'Black People'. Some scholars identify solely by reference to the Country and People to whom they belong. Without taking a position on what is a complicated and nuanced debate, I have used all terms throughout this book.

The second issue concerns the scope of the analysis. There are many commonalities between the historical experiences of Indigenous women in Australia and North America. All have suffered the lingering effects of dispossession, child removal policies and systemic discrimination in the criminal justice system. This book, however, is confined to the outlaw culture of Indigenous women in Australia. It is anticipated that later work will have a broader compass, so that it will be inclusive of the experiences of Indigenous women outside of Australia.

This book will be divided into three substantive parts. The first, in Chapter 2, will discuss the history and fundamental precepts of CRT and critical race feminism ('CRF'). It is within the latter theory that Black women's outlaw culture sits. This chapter will also identify parallels between the racial hierarchies in Australia and the United States of America, before considering the work of scholars who have adopted the principles of CRT to illuminate the omnipresence of racism in Australia.

Chapter 3 will begin by discussing the nexus between demeaning representations of Indigenous women and colonisation. It will go on to introduce Indigenous women's outlaw culture. Narratives of outlaw women are recorded in memoirs, oral histories and testimony to inquiries. Finally, I will argue that judgments are potential sources of information about outlaw culture. The stories of Indigenous women are usually absent from the text of judgments. However, the experiences of Indigenous women who emerge in judgments can be contextualised by departmental records, historical analyses and oral stories within Indigenous communities. When such narratives are pieced together, it is possible to find instances of outlaw culture.

Finally, Chapter 4 will provide an example of the application of the methodology discussed in Chapter 3. By drawing upon archival materials, historical accounts of the Queensland frontier and newspaper articles, I will imagine the story of the early outlaw woman, Eliza Woree. Eliza featured prominently in the backdrop to the decision of the Supreme Court of Queensland in *Dempsey v Rigg*.[12] In December 1913, Isaac Rigg employed Eliza to perform washing and ironing. As Rigg had failed to obtain a permit to employ her, he was charged with the offence of unlawfully employing an Aboriginal under s. 14 of the *Aboriginals Protection and Restriction of the Sale of Opium Act 1897* (Qld).[13]

Two months earlier Eliza had married Joe Andrews, who was a 'Malay' and a 'native of Batavia'.[14] Rigg argued that because Eliza married an 'alien' she had lost her Australian nationality. It followed that Eliza ceased to be an Aboriginal within the meaning of the *Aboriginals Protection and Restriction of the Sale of Opium Act 1897* (Qld). The Supreme Court of Queensland disagreed. Eliza continued to be subject to the Act, and therefore, Isaac Rigg was liable under s 14.

Although she was at the centre of the factual scenario, Eliza Woree's story was absent from the judgments of the Supreme Court of Queensland. Her opinions and aspirations were utterly irrelevant to the men who

[12] *Dempsey v Rigg* [1914] St R Qd 245.

[13] The relationship between 'protection' and the availability of opium was explained by Queensland's Secretary of Agriculture in his Second Reading of the Aboriginals Protection and Restriction of the Sale of Opium Bill: 'As a matter of fact, to deal with the aboriginals on the ordinary basis of dealing with our own people is not a wise or a just proceeding ... In order to give them the protection they ought to have it is necessary to treat them very much as if they were children. This Bill proposes to prohibit the indiscriminate use of opium, which has hitherto operated to the extreme detriment of the aboriginals; it also embodies some of the clauses already contained in our licensing laws prohibiting the sale of liquor to aboriginals. The remaining portion of the Bill provides for the establishment of suitable reserves for the use of aboriginals, under the charge of officers appointed as protectors, and takes power to require aboriginals to reside on those reserves, so that they may be kept away as far as possible from the evil effects produced by going about near hotels and other places, where they may get liquor or opium. See Queensland, *Parliamentary Debates*, Legislative Council, 7 December 1897, 1887 (The Secretary for Agriculture).

[14] *Dempsey v Rigg* [1914] St R Qd 245, 246. Batavia is now known as Jakarta.

wielded so much power over her life. This chapter will piece together her story. It will begin with Eliza's childhood, which coincided with the invasion of the Bama of tropical north Queensland. This chapter will consider how the Act and the common law later impacted upon crucial aspects of Eliza's life, namely, marriage, employment and her nationality.

Finally, this chapter will imagine Eliza's story after the Supreme Court's decision. Although there is much still unknown about her life, we can be confident that Eliza was a determined and resourceful woman. At a time when all women were denied agency, Eliza achieved the remarkable feat of creating a life of her own. Within 6 years of the Supreme Court's decision, Eliza had left her husband and was living in 'Malaytown', an informal settlement on the outskirts of Cairns. Tragically, her intelligence and fierce independence would be the very qualities that would attract the attention of the authorities, who condemned Eliza to spend the remainder of her life in the penal settlement of Palm Island.

This book will conclude by arguing that now more than ever, it is crucial that scholars and students unearth the stories of the Indigenous women who have been at the vanguard of outlaw culture. At a time when the world is finally beginning to grasp the message that Black lives matter, it is imperative that we pause to hear the voices of Indigenous women who created spaces of sanctuary from the violence of a world that deemed them unworthy of the law's protection. Such stories matter because Indigenous women's lives matter.

CHAPTER 2

Critical Race Theory, Critical Race Feminism and the Stories of Outsiders

Abstract This chapter provides the theoretical foundations for the following chapters. It identifies the precepts of critical race theory ('CRT') and critical race feminism ('CRF'). The chapter introduces the work of scholars such as Monica J. Evans and Regina Austin on Black women's outlaw culture. It also casts light on similarities between racism in Australia and the United States of America. Finally, the chapter acknowledges the work of Australian scholars who are extending CRT to illuminate the pervasiveness of racism in Australian society.

Keywords Critical race theory · Critical race feminism · Storytelling · Indigenous Australians

Introduction

When I was six years old, I believed that my father's study was the most fascinating place in the world. I was intrigued by the electric typewriter from which he composed his important business. It sat on a desk that was surrounded by old furniture, worn out appliances and family keepsakes. One day I noticed a sign among the clutter which bore the name, 'Nigger Creek'. We never discussed the origins of that sign, or how it came to be

N. Watson, *Aboriginal Women, Law and Critical Race Theory*, Palgrave Studies in Race, Ethnicity, Indigeneity and Criminal Justice,
https://doi.org/10.1007/978-3-030-87327-1_2

in our house. But I like to imagine my father tearing it down in the middle of the night and stealing away in our old panel van.

As I grew older, I learnt that Queensland is dotted with places that have names like Nigger Creek. Sites such as Skull Hole and Skeleton Creek are among the scant reminders of the extraordinary violence with which Indigenous people were dispossessed of their lands.[1] Likewise, there are few memorials that pay homage to the stories of those who met brutal ends on the Queensland frontier. A rare exception is 'The Leap' in the Pioneer Valley, a place that took its name from the death of an Indigenous woman in the 1860s.

Following the discovery of speared cattle,[2] the Native Police set out to conduct a 'dispersal'. The term 'dispersal' was a euphemism in nineteenth-century Queensland for the arbitrary slaughter of Indigenous people.[3] Together with her infant daughter, the woman sought sanctuary on the summit of what is now known as Mount Mandurana. Perhaps realising that it was only a matter of time before the Native Police captured them, she leapt, taking her child with her.[4] According to legend, the child miraculously survived and was reared by settlers.[5] Today, a pub called The Leap Hotel sits at the foot of the mountain. In the front stands a statue of the mother who perished, who was named 'Kowaha'.[6]

Little is known of the narratives of other Indigenous women who suffered a similar fate to that of Kowaha. Their invisibility is an opening to one of the great concerns of CRT scholars, which is the power relations that underlie the stories that shape social reality. Stories that define a nation's history and the values that inform societal norms invariably

[1] Jonathan Richards, ''Many Were Killed from Falling Over the Cliffs': The Naming of Mount Wheeler, Central Queensland' in Ian D. Clark, Luise Hercus and Laura Kostanski (eds), *Indigenous and Minority Placenames: Australian and International Perspectives* (ANU Press, 2014), 147, 150.

[2] Clive Moore, 'Blackgin's Leap: A Window into Aboriginal-European Relations in the Pioneer Valley, Queensland in the 1860s' (1990) 14(1/2) *Aboriginal History*, 61, 65.

[3] Jonathan Richards, *The Secret War: A True History of Queensland's Native Police* (University of Queensland Press, 2008), 77.

[4] Moore (n 2), 61.

[5] Ibid.

[6] Mick Roberts, 'The North Queensland Pub Named After the Tragic Death of Aboriginal Woman, Kowaha' *Time Gents: Australian Pub Project* (Blog Post, 7 February 2021), https://timegents.com/2021/02/07/the-north-queensland-pub-named-after-the-tragic-death-of-aboriginal-woman-kowaha/.

belong to dominant groups. Critical race scholars counteract such narratives with the stories of those within marginalised communities. The narratives of individuals such as Kowaha have the power to disrupt the status quo. They shatter the myth of peaceful settlement and cast light on the fortitude of the many Black women who actively resisted their oppressors.

This chapter will be divided into four parts. Part one will introduce the foundational principles of CRT, with a particular focus on outsider storytelling. Part two will discuss the precepts of critical race feminism ('CRF') before exploring outlaw culture. Part three will identify some parallels between the experiences of Indigenous people in Australia and the conditions that sparked the emergence of CRT in the United States of America ('USA'). Finally, part four will introduce the work of scholars who are extending CRT to an Australian context.

Part One: Critical Race Theory

Introduction

The collective of academics who wrote the foundational scholarship of CRT came together in the closing decades of the twentieth century, out of recognition that despite some impressive civil rights victories such as *Brown v Board of Education*,[7] little had improved for the vast majority of African Americans. Decades after the *Brown* decision declared segregation in public education to be unconstitutional, Black children were still attending schools that were 'racially isolated and inferior'.[8] At the same time a stock story had taken hold, according to which, the goal of equality had been realised.

Drawing inspiration from critical legal studies and radical feminism,[9] the founders of CRT sought to cast light on the lived realities of people of colour. The 'intellectual father figure'[10] of CRT was Derrick Bell, who had already contributed much to the legal battle to break segregation

[7] 347 U.S. 483 (1954).

[8] Derrick A. Bell Jr, '*Brown v Board of Education* and the Interest-Convergence Dilemma' (1979–1980) 93(3) *Harvard Law Review*, 518.

[9] Richard Delgado and Jean Stefancic, *Critical Race Theory: An Introduction* (New York University Press, 3rd ed, 2017), 5.

[10] Ibid., 6.

before pursuing an academic career.[11] As the former Assistant Counsel for the National Association for the Advancement of Colored People Legal Defense and Educational Fund, Bell had supervised hundreds of desegregation cases, concerning schools and restaurant chains.[12] Bell was not only a champion of the civil rights movement, he was also the first African American to become a tenured professor at Harvard Law School.[13] Together with scholars such as Richard Delgado, Charles Lawrence, Mari Matsuda, Kimberlé Crenshaw, Patricia Williams, Cheryl Harris and others, Bell produced the movement's foundational scholarship.

Today, the antecedents of CRT are contested, with some scholars tracing its origins back to the work of Black women abolitionists[14] and the writings of W. E. B. Du Bois.[15] What is beyond doubt, however, is the far-reaching impact of this revolutionary movement. Critical race theory has spread from the legal academy to other disciplines, including social work, psychology and education. It has also inspired offshoots, such as LatCrit, AsianCrit and QueerRaceCrit,[16] and has been embraced by scholars around the world.

One of the tenets of CRT is that racism is omnipresent. It is a 'relentless, daily fact of life' that is so enmeshed in America's legal and political systems that is it 'nearly unrecognizable'.[17] Racism manifests in overt actions and subtle gestures. While the former is often proscribed by antidiscrimination laws, people of colour have little protection against the harms caused by covert forms of racism, such as institutional racism and

[11] Adrien Katherine Wing, 'Space Traders for the Twenty-First Century' (2009) 11 *Berkeley Journal of African-American Law and Policy*, 49, 50.

[12] 'Derrick Bell (1930–2011): An Iconoclast and a Community Builder' *Harvard Law Today*, 6 October 2011, https://today.law.harvard.edu/derrick-bell-1930-2011/.

[13] Ibid.

[14] Latoya Johnson, 'From the Anti-Slavery Movement to Now: (RE) Examining the Relationship Between Critical Race Theory and Black Feminist Thought' (2015) 22(3–4) *Race, Gender and Class*, 227

[15] Kamau Rashid, '"To Break Asunder Along the Lesions of Race". The Critical Race Theory of W.E.B. Du Bois' (2011) 14(5) *Race, Ethnicity and Education*, 585.

[16] Adrien Katherine Wing, 'Introduction' in Adrien Katherine Wing (ed), *Critical Race Feminism: A Reader* (New York University Press, 2nd ed, 2003), 1, 5.

[17] André Douglas Pond Cummings, 'A Furious Kinship: Critical Race Theory and the Hip-Hop Nation' in Richard Delgado and Jean Stefancic (eds), *Critical Race Theory: The Cutting Edge* (Temple University Press, 3rd ed, 2013), 107, 108.

microaggressions. The latter have been defined as 'subtle, stunning, often automatic ... exchanges which are 'put downs' of Blacks by offenders'.[18]

Critical race theory posits that due to histories of slavery and segregation, and the ongoing pervasiveness of racism, people of colour have a unique voice.[19] Another precept of CRT is the 'social construction thesis'.[20] In the absence of a 'biological or genetic reality,'[21] races are categories that are socially constructed. Critical race scholars argue that race should be understood as a 'power system that creates privileges in some and disadvantages in others'.[22] The characteristics shared by members of privileged groups are treated as societal norms, but those within such groups are often unaware of their advantages.

Critical race scholars also seek to expose the futility of 'colorblindness,'[23] the notion that racism has been virtually eradicated. Only the most egregious manifestations of racism fall within the ambit of anti-discrimination laws, while everyday racism rarely attracts censure. Critical race scholars share a discontentment with liberalism, which has been characterised by an unwavering faith in the legal system and contentment with incremental reform.[24] But CRT scholars do not argue that rights are unimportant. To reject rights as irrelevant is to diminish the lived experience of Black people, whose histories of political action have largely revolved around calls for the extension of rights.[25]

[18] Pierce cited in Chavella T. Pittman, 'Racial Microaggressions: The Narratives of African American Faculty at a Predominantly White University' (2012) 81(1) *Journal of Negro Education*, 82, 83.

[19] Johnson (n 14), 239.

[20] Wing (n 16), 5.

[21] Delgado and Stefancic cited by Johnson (n 14), 239.

[22] Stephanie M. Wildman and Adrienne D. Davis, 'Language and Silence: Making Systems of Privilege Visible' in Richard Delgado and Jean Stefancic (eds), *Critical Race Theory: The Cutting Edge* (Temple University Press, 3rd ed, 2013), 794, 795.

[23] Johnson (n 14), 238.

[24] Richard Delgado and Jean Stefancic (eds), *Critical Race Theory: The Cutting Edge* (Temple University Press, 3rd ed, 2013), 6.

[25] Patricia J. Williams, 'Alchemical Notes: Reconstructing Ideals from Deconstructed Rights' in Richard Delgado and Jean Stefancic (eds), *Critical Race Theory: The Cutting Edge* (Temple University Press, 3rd ed, 2013), 97, 101.

Bell considered that racism was a perpetual feature of American society.[26] His argument was grounded in the reality that by the 1980s, many of the triumphs of the civil rights movement had been reduced to fleeting 'peaks of progress', which had eventually slid into 'irrelevance'.[27] Legalised segregation may have come to an end, but the vast majority of Black Americans remained mired in socio-economic disadvantage. Bell called for a realistic approach to avoid despair and allow for the creation of strategies that acknowledged the permanence of racism.[28]

Another tenet of CRT is Bell's 'interest convergence' theory,[29] according to which, decisions such as *Brown* are only ever possible when the relief sought by African Americans also serves the interests of those at the apex of the racial hierarchy.[30] Such victories are likely to be symbolic rather than substantive, and are valued as proof of society's commitment to racial equality.[31] Bell's theory drew support from the scholar, Mary L. Dudziak whose work revealed how *Brown* served the interests of American foreign policy during the Cold War.[32] At the time of the decision, newspapers around the world were exposing the discrimination encountered by non-White foreign dignitaries on American soil.[33] Such coverage played into the hands of America's enemies. The *Brown* decision was a powerful tool to deflect such attention.

Scholars who adhere to CRT seek to unite theory with practice, out of recognition that the traditional model of academic scholarship has always been detached from the injustices endured by those who lack power.[34] They also subscribe to the view that the struggle against racism must be fought alongside resistance against sexism, homophobia and other forms

[26] Derrick Bell, 'Racial Realism' (1992) 24(2) *Connecticut Law Review*, 363, 373–374.

[27] Ibid.

[28] Ibid., 377.

[29] Bell (n 8), 523.

[30] Derrick Bell, *Race, Racism and American Law* (Little, Brown and Company, 2nd ed, 1980), 7.

[31] Ibid.

[32] Mary L. Dudziak, 'Desegregation as a Cold War Imperative' in Richard Delgado and Jean Stefancic (eds), *Critical Race Theory: The Cutting Edge* (Temple University Press, 3rd ed, 2013), 136.

[33] Ibid., 138.

[34] Adrien K. Wing, 'Is There a Future for Critical Race Theory?' (2016) 66(1) *Journal of Legal Education*, 44, 48–49.

of subjugation.[35] Finally, CRT scholars often take a multi-disciplinary approach; injecting insights from history, African American studies and other fields into their work.[36]

Outsider Storytelling

One of the methodologies used by CRT scholars is storytelling. Social reality is largely constructed by narratives. Such narratives can clothe inequality with the appearance of normality or present the status quo as the best possible outcome in a world that is unavoidably unjust. Critical race scholars challenge such narratives with the stories of those who live in marginalised communities.

Scholars who engage with the stories of outsiders argue that they are a 'powerful means for destroying mind-set – the bundle of presuppositions, received wisdoms, and shared understandings against a background of which legal and political discourse takes place'.[37] They also have resonance for scholars who come from communities that are reliant upon oral storytelling as a means of transferring important histories from one generation to the next.[38] Finally, storytelling is a valuable medium because of its accessibility. As distinct from law journals, stories are accessible to audiences outside of the Academy.

Critical race scholars often begin their work with a powerful story in which a loved one was a protagonist. In the introduction to a seminal piece, Cheryl Harris described how her fair-complexioned grandmother 'passed' to gain employment in a retail store in the 1930s.[39] Each morning, Harris' grandmother left her home in the Black side of town and boarded a bus alongside other Black passengers. While at work, however, she suppressed her identity, and even held her silence as her

[35] Pond Cummings (n 17), 108.

[36] Wing (n 34), 48.

[37] Richard Delgado, 'Storytelling for Oppositionists and Others: A Plea for Narrative' in Richard Delgado and Jean Stefancic (eds), *Critical Race Theory: The Cutting Edge* (Temple University Press, 3rd ed, 2013), 72.

[38] Wing (n 16), 6.

[39] Cheryl I. Harris, 'Whiteness as Property' (1993) 106(8) *Harvard Law Review*, 1710.

colleagues made racist remarks. Overwhelmed by the strain of hiding her identity, Harris' grandmother eventually left her employment.[40]

Such stories are not only shocking but moving. They linger in the reader's mind for days, if not years afterwards. It was long ago that I first read Harris's article, but every so often, I find myself thinking about her grandmother and the extraordinary sacrifice that she made in order to provide for her family. The story is also a metaphor for Harris' thesis that whiteness and property are intertwined. The appropriation of Native American lands and the slavery of African Americans were both supported by a racialised conception of property, which was legitimised by law.[41] Whiteness signalled not only the ability to possess land and own others. It also conferred lifelong protection from ever becoming an object of property. After the abolition of slavery, whiteness continued to shape one's entire life trajectory:

> Whiteness determined whether one could vote, travel freely, attend schools, obtain work, and indeed, defined the structure of social relations along the entire spectrum of interactions between the individual and society.[42]

In addition to transforming legal scholarship through the inclusion of outsider stories, the pioneers of CRT also wrote innovative legal fiction. Arguably, the most renowned work of legal fiction is Derrick Bell's *Chronicle of the Space Traders*.[43] The story begins with the arrival of intergalactic visitors, who have a bargain to strike with the American people. In exchange for solutions to the nation's debt, environmental and energy crises, the aliens seek to take all African Americans back to their home star. The stunned earthlings are given sixteen days to mull over the proposal. During that time various groups consider how their particular interests could be advanced by a possible trade. On the final day, which happens to be the Martin Luther King holiday, the nation calls upon African Americans to perform their patriotic duty. Mirroring the experiences of their ancestors, African Americans are sent to an uncertain future on the alien

[40] Ibid., 1711.

[41] Ibid., 1715.

[42] Ibid., 1745.

[43] Derrick A. Bell Jr, 'After We're Gone: Prudent Speculations on American in a Postracial Epoch' in Richard Delgado and Jean Stefancic (eds), *Critical Race Theory: The Cutting Edge* (Temple University Press, 3rd ed, 2013), 9, 10.

ships. Apart from being an entertaining story, Bell's story was a clever allegory for America's racial hierarchy, and the nation's long history of sacrificing those on the bottom rung.

Part Two: Critical Race Feminism

Introduction

While CRT was embraced by many Black women legal scholars, some acknowledged that it was not always inclusive of women of colour.[44] The stories of Black women were similarly missing from feminist theory and conventional rights jurisprudence. Critical race feminism (CRF) emerged out of recognition of this absence, and the need for a jurisprudence that was informed by the voices of women of colour. This part will identify the core principles of CRF before turning to outlaw culture.

Critical race feminists subscribe to some of the tenets of CRT, such as the ubiquity of racism and the use of storytelling as methodology. However, CRF scholars have also developed their own intellectual tools. First and foremost, CRF scholars place the voices of women of colour at the centre of their analysis. Critical race feminists are also concerned with the legal treatment of women of colour throughout the world.[45]

Critical race feminists have embraced anti-essentialism, which contests the belief that identities are 'stable, constant or separable'.[46] They also argue that gender essentialism, that is, the notion that there is one uniform female voice, and racial essentialism which posits a universal Black experience, both fragment the lives of Black women who are subject to multiple forms of oppression.[47] Related to anti-essentialism is the concept

[44] Adrien Katherine Wing, 'Critical Race Feminism and the International Human Rights of Women in Bosnia, Palestine, and South Africa: Issues for LatCrit Theory' (1996/1997) 28(2) *University of Miami Inter-American Law Review*, 337, 340.

[45] Ibid., 341.

[46] Lori D. Patton and LaWanda W. Ward, 'Missing Black Undergraduate Women and the Politics of Disposability: A Critical Race Feminist Perspective' (2016) 85(3) *Journal of Negro Education*, 330, 331.

[47] Angela P. Harris, 'Race and Essentialism in Feminist Legal Theory' in Adrien Katherine Wing (ed), *Critical Race Feminism: A Reader* (New York University Press, 2nd ed, 2003), 34.

of intersectionality, a term coined by Professor Kimberlé Crenshaw.[48] Intersectionality is the notion that individuals have intersecting or coinciding identities which shape their daily lives.[49] Critical race feminists recognise that Black women are marginalised at multiple, overlapping points—race, gender, class, sexuality and sometimes 'as Black women'.[50] Due to the 'single axis approach'[51] of the law it is ill-equipped to respond to the intersectional lives of Black women, and therefore, many of the injustices that they suffer are unnamed.

In addition to bringing women of colour to the centre of their analysis, CRF scholars have shed light on the latent injuries that result from racism. For example, Professor Patricia Williams created the term 'spirit murder', which is a 'disregard for others whose lives qualitatively depend upon our regard'.[52] The impacts of spirit murder are so devastating that it is 'no less than the equivalent of body murder'.[53] Racism is but one manifestation of spirit murder, which may also take the form of 'cultural obliteration, prostitution, abandonment of the elderly and the homeless, and genocide'.[54] Thousands of words have been devoted to the concept of spirit murder since it was devised by Professor Williams three decades ago. One recent application concerned the relentless microaggressions confronted by Black female professors in American universities that took the form of character assassination, disparagement of course content and demeaning assumptions about their professional competency.[55]

[48] Kimberlé Crenshaw, 'Demarginalizing the Intersection of Race and Sex' (1989) *University of Chicago Legal Forum*, 139.

[49] Johnson (n 14), 235.

[50] Crenshaw (n 48), 149.

[51] Patton and Ward (n 46), 331.

[52] Patricia Williams, 'Spirit Murdering the Messenger: The Discourse of Fingerpointing as the Law's Response to Racism' (1987) 42(1) *University of Miami Law Review*, 127, 151.

[53] Ibid.

[54] Ibid.

[55] Jemimah L. Young and Dorothy E. Hines, 'Killing My Spirit, Renewing My Soul: Black Female Professors' Critical Reflections on Spirit Killings while Teaching' (2018) 6(1) *Women, Gender, and Families of Color*, 18.

Black Women and Outlaw Culture

It is within this body of CRF scholarship that Monica J. Evans' piece, 'Stealing Away: Black Women, Outlaw Culture and the Rhetoric of Rights'[56] sits. Evans begins her article with the lyrics of an old spiritual that slaves in the Antebellum South would sing to signal to others that the time for escape was near. Their oppressors, who considered them to be mere 'beasts of burden',[57] were oblivious to the lyrics' ulterior purpose. Today, such practices can be viewed as the forerunners of a positive outlaw culture that provides a sanctuary from the 'terrifying exclusion' of Black people from the protection of the law.[58]

Historically, the figure of the outlaw has been portrayed as male. Writing about lawbreakers within Black communities, Regina Austin argues that there has always been a 'subtle admiration' for male criminals who rely upon their wits to evade a punitive and unjust legal system.[59] Female outlaws, however, have typically received no such empathy, with their actions often being condemned as 'unfeminine'.[60] This disavowal of Black women lawbreakers overlooks the contributions of those who have transformed the concept of an outlaw from the 'dominant paradigm of lawless anarchy' into a 'culturally-embedded strategy for resistance'.[61]

Evans defines outlaw culture as 'a network of shared institutions, values and practices through which subordinated groups elaborate an autonomous, oppositional consciousness'.[62] Those values and practices are manifest in a spectrum of relationships with the law. At one end are the lawbreakers, for whom illegality is inextricably tied to empowerment. On the other are those who create alternatives to their oppression through stringent compliance with the law.

[56] Monica J. Evans, 'Stealing Away: Black Women, Outlaw Culture and the Rhetoric of Rights' (1993) 28(2) *Harvard Civil Rights-Civil Liberties Law Review*, 263.

[57] Ibid., 264.

[58] Ibid., 265.

[59] Regina Austin, '"The Black Community," It Lawbreakers, and a Politics of Identification' (1992) 65(4) *Southern California Law Review*, 1769, 1776.

[60] Ibid., 1792.

[61] Evans (n 56), 271.

[62] Ibid., 268 (footnotes omitted).

Evans describes Harriet Tubman as an outlaw in the 'truest sense'.[63] After escaping from slavery in Maryland via the Underground Railroad, Tubman established links with abolitionists in the North. Throughout the 1850s, she returned to the South on 19 occasions, thereby securing freedom for hundreds of people.[64] Later, she devoted herself to the Union cause; tending to wounded soldiers and drawing upon her knowledge of the Underground Railroad to become a spy.[65]

In contrast, the Black Clubwomen of the late nineteenth and twentieth centuries sought sanctuary through faithful adherence to the law. The Clubwomen created social welfare programs that included schools, kindergartens and aged care homes. In addition to providing spaces of safety, the Clubwomen also countered harmful stereotypes revolving around Black female sexuality by representing themselves as 'largely de-sexualized, well-educated and hyper-respectable Victorian ladies'.[66]

In 1896, the Clubwomen united under the banner of the National Association of Colored Women ('NACW').[67] Under the adage of 'Lifting as We Climb'[68] its middle-class members focused on improving the lives of the most disadvantaged members of Black communities. Later, the NACW campaigned against lynching,[69] and the sexual exploitation of Black women.[70] The Clubwomen were not driven by 'atomistic individualism,'[71] but rather, an appreciation that the struggle for rights had little meaning if it did not also foster communal bonds.[72]

In summary, CRT emerged in the closing decades of the twentieth century, out of recognition that despite stunning legal victories such as

[63] Ibid., 272.

[64] Kahlil Chism, 'Harriet Tubman: Spy, Veteran, and Widow' (2005) 19(2) *OAH Magazine of History*, 47.

[65] Ibid.

[66] Evans (n 56), 284.

[67] Amii Larkin Barnard, 'The Application of Critical Race Feminism to the Anti-Lynching Movement. Black Women's Fight against Race and Gender Ideology', 1892–1920' (1993) 3 *UCLA Women's Law Journal*, 1, 22.

[68] Ibid.

[69] Ibid., 23.

[70] Ibid., 25.

[71] Evans (n 56), 296.

[72] Ibid.

Brown v Board of Education, America's racial hierarchy remained largely intact. Critical race scholars argue that racism is ever-present, and perhaps, even permanent. Critical race scholars illuminate the pervasiveness of racism by privileging the stories of outsiders. Critical race feminists have strengthened CRT scholarship by creating new intellectual tools, such as intersectionality, which recognises that women of colour are disempowered at various, coinciding points, such as gender, race, class and sexuality. Within CRF is the work of scholars such as Regina Austin and Monica J. Evans on female outlaws. The latter argues that Black women have reformed the concept of an 'outlaw' into a body of practices, values and tactics for the realisation of empowerment and protection.

Part Three: Commonalities Between the United States of America and Australia

Introduction

This part will advocate for greater engagement with CRT by scholars who work in the field of Indigenous studies, out of recognition of three commonalities between Australia and the USA. Firstly, in common with the USA, Australian society has been divided into a racial hierarchy since the advent of colonisation. Secondly, any advancements made by Indigenous people have been preceded by long and arduous campaigns. Over time, however, those gains have lost significance. Finally, it will be argued that like the USA, racism in contemporary Australian society is pervasive.

The Racial Hierarchy

For thousands of years prior to the arrival of the British, Australia was a mosaic of countries that were home to hundreds of Indigenous nations. Countries emerged out of journeys undertaken by ancestral beings during the creation period known as the 'Dreaming'. The ancestors created the physical features of the land, and narratives so that the people could live in accordance with the law.[73] The journeys undertaken by the ancestors during the creation period remain etched in song lines that traverse

[73] Christine Judith Nicholls, '"Dreamings" and Dreaming Narratives: What's the relationship?' *The Conversation* (online, 6 February 2014), https://theconversation.com/dreamings-and-dreaming-narratives-whats-the-relationship-20837.

the continent. Song lines are 'mnemonic methods' of storing detailed knowledge about the histories and features of the land.[74]

The settlers were ill-equipped to understand either the land or the complex and highly evolved societies that they would come to dispossess. We know from their written observations that the settlers were struck by the beauty of lands that they compared to 'gentleman's parks' in England.[75] The belief that the environment was pristine rather than the outcome of thousands of years of Indigenous stewardship, was but one that would provide a rationale for the invasion. Another was the assigned inferiority of Indigenous people. Representations of Indigenous people as primitive and child-like enabled settler society to be structured on racial lines. At the apex were settlers who forged a national identity out of a shared commitment to racial homogeneity, and a belief in an 'extended community of British peoples'.[76] On the bottom rung were Indigenous people, considered to be so 'barbarous' and 'so entirely destitute ... of the rudest forms of civil polity'[77] that their ageless bonds with their lands were utterly disregarded.

Although deemed to be British subjects, Indigenous people were often excluded from the protection of the law. In my home state of Queensland, the rule of law was suspended as the Native Police embarked on a decades-long slaughter of Indigenous people. The Native Police operated at the behest of the Commissioners of Crown Lands,[78] before becoming a separate unit under the control of the Commissioner of Police in 1864.[79] In his memoir, *The Black Police of Queensland*,[80] the former Native Police

[74] Diana James, 'Signposted by Song: Cultural Routes of the Australian Desert,' (2013) 25(3) *Historic Environment*, 30, 33.

[75] Bill Gammage, *The Biggest Estate on Earth: How Aborigines Made Australia* (Allen & Unwin, 2011), 6.

[76] Matthew Jordan, '"Not on Your Life": Cabinet and Liberalisation of the White Australia Policy, 1964–67' (2018) 46(1) *The Journal of Imperial and Commonwealth History*, 169, 170.

[77] *Mabo v State of Queensland* (No 2) (1992), 175 CLR 1, 40 (Brennan J)

[78] Kathy Frankland, 'A Brief History of Government Administration of Aboriginal and Torres Strait Islander Peoples in Queensland', https://www.slq.qld.gov.au/sites/default/files/www.slq.qld.gov.au/__data/assets/pdf_file/0008/93734/admin_history_aboriginal_and_torres_strait_islanders.pdf, 1.

[79] Ibid.

[80] Edward B. Kennedy, *The Black Police of Queensland: Reminiscences of Official Work and Adventures of the Early Days of the Colony* (Murray, 1902).

Officer, Edward B. Kennedy described a force that consisted of small units of Aboriginal troopers, who were led by white men. As the frontier moved throughout the colony detachments conducted 'dispersals'; a euphemism for indiscriminate murder.[81] The Native Police was responsible for so much of the violence on the frontier, but its officers and troopers did not act in isolation. Settlers also used a variety of means to erase Indigenous people from the very lands that had belonged to them for an eternity. Arguably the most abominable was the 'death-pudding'—flour laced with arsenic or strychnine.[82]

As individuals from Asia, Africa and the Pacific Islands came to Australia's shores, they too suffered the brunt of settler xenophobia. In 1901 the new Commonwealth Parliament sought to legislate to exclude all non-White immigration. However, members were at variance on how this goal was to be achieved. Some, like the Labor Party leader, John C. Watson, sought an express prohibition of anyone who was 'an aboriginal native of Asia, Africa, or of the islands thereof'.[83] Such an explicit racial exclusion had the potential to damage Australia's relations with its Asian neighbours, and cause international embarrassment for Great Britain. In the end, the Parliament created an indirect means of excluding potential non-White immigrants by way of a dictation test, which could be delivered in any European language. The test, which materialised in s. 3(a) *Immigration Restriction Act 1901* (Cth), was but one element of the White Australia Policy, which continued to evolve until the latter part of the twentieth century.[84]

Non-Europeans were subject to a raft of discriminatory measures, which resounded in social security legislation. For example, the *Invalid*

[81] Amanda Nettelbeck and Lyndall Ryan, 'Salutary Lessons: Native Police and the "Civilising" Role of Legalised Violence in Colonial Australia' (2018) 46(1) *The Journal of Imperial and Commonwealth History*, 47, 56–57.

[82] Raymond Evans, Kay Saunders and Kathryn Cronin, *Exclusion, Exploitation and Extermination: Race Relations in Colonial Queensland* (University of Queensland Press, 1993), 49.

[83] David Atkinson, 'The White Australia Policy, the British Empire, and the World' (2015) Department of History Faculty Publications, Purdue University, Paper 4, https://docs.lib.purdue.edu/cgi/viewcontent.cgi?article=1004&context=histpubs.

[84] Andrew Markus, 'Of Continuities and Discontinuities: Reflections on a Century of Australian Immigration Control' in Laksiri Jayasuriya, David Walker and Jan Gothard (eds), *Legacies of White Australia: Race, Culture and Nation* (University of Western Australia Press, 2003), 175, 176.

and Old-Age Pensions Act 1908 (Cth) rendered persons who were 'Asiatics (except those born in Australia), or aboriginal natives of Australia, Africa, the Islands of the Pacific, or New Zealand,'[85] ineligible to receive an old-age pension. The maternity allowance was similarly denied to mothers who were 'Asiatics' or 'aboriginal natives of Australia, Papua, or the Islands of the Pacific'.[86] According to Professor John Murphy, it was not until 1966 that Australian welfare law became entirely free of racial exclusions.[87]

Short-Lived Peaks of Progress

Since the latter part of the twentieth century, the laws and policies that leave indelible impacts upon Indigenous lives have swung like a pendulum between precious moments of hope and those of deep despair. Progress for Indigenous people has largely consisted of brief victories that emerged out of long and arduous campaigns. With the passage of time those bitterly contested gains have lost momentum.

One such milestone was the successful 1967 referendum, which resulted in the amendment of s. 51(xxvi) of the *Australian Constitution*, enabling the Commonwealth to make laws in relation to Aboriginal people. It also led to the deletion of s. 127, which had prevented Aboriginal people from being included in the census. Almost ninety per cent of the Australian electorate voted 'yes'[88] to the reforms, in what is now recognised as the beginning of a more enlightened approach to Indigenous affairs.

The successful referendum was the culmination of decades of activism, including a 10-year campaign by the multi-racial organisation, the Federal Council for Aboriginal Advancement, which would later be known as the Federal Council for the Advancement of Aborigines and Torres Strait Islanders.[89] But in the aftermath of this extraordinary victory little

[85] *Invalid and Old-Age Pensions Act 1908* (Cth) s. 16(1)(c).

[86] *Maternity Allowance Act 1912* (Cth) s. 6(2).

[87] John Murphy, 'Conditional Inclusion: Aborigines and Welfare Rights in Australia, 1900–47' (2013) 44(2) *Australian Historical Studies*, 206, 207.

[88] George Williams, 'The Races Power and the 1967 Referendum' (2007) 11 *Australian Indigenous Law Review*, 8, 9.

[89] Russell McGregor, 'Another Nation: Aboriginal Activism in the Late 1960s and Early 1970s' (2009) 40(3) *Australian Historical Studies*, 343, 346.

changed on the ground, fuelling widespread disillusionment. Such sentiments were shared by the prominent 'yes' vote campaigner, Oodgeroo Noonuccal, who claimed that the referendum delivered few benefits to Indigenous people, and had merely 'eased the guilty conscience of white Australians'.[90]

It was not until the election of the Whitlam Government in 1972 that Indigenous people were given reason for optimism. The Whitlam Government embarked on a crucial reform program under the banner of self-determination. In 1973 the Commonwealth established an elected Indigenous advisory body, the National Aboriginal Consultative Committee and the first stand-alone department for Aboriginal affairs.[91] A degree of safety from unlawful discrimination would also be provided by the *Racial Discrimination Act 1975* (Cth). The Whitlam Government was dismissed from office in 1975. However, its successor, the Fraser Government would continue many of its initiatives, such as Australia's first federal land rights legislation, the *Aboriginal Land Rights (Northern Territory) Act 1976* (Cth).

In the final decade of the twentieth century, Australia finally received its equivalent to *Brown v Board of Education* in *Mabo v State of Queensland (No 2)*.[92] In recognising the native title of the plaintiffs, the majority of the High Court overturned the application of the doctrine of terra nullius. Even though *Mabo* was a watershed, it did little to disrupt the impacts of two centuries of dispossession. The comments of Professor Michael Dodson soon after the High Court handed down its decision were strikingly prophetic:

> The *Mabo* decision does not recognise equality of rights or equality of entitlement: It recognises the legal validity of Aboriginal title until the white man wants that land...

[90] Ibid., 347.

[91] Marcia Langton, 'Koowarta: A Warrior for Justice: A Brief History of Queensland's Racially Discriminatory Legislation and the Aboriginal Litigants Who Fought It' (2014) 23(1) *Griffith Law Review*, 16, 26.

[92] (1992) 175 CLR 1.

> For the vast majority of Indigenous Australians the *Mabo* decision is a belated act of sterile symbolism. It will not return the country of our ancestors, nor will it result in compensation for its loss.[93]

Although the subsequent *Native Title Act 1993* (Cth) created a process for the recognition of native title, many of its provisions are concerned with insulating established property rights and future land management from the recognition of native title.[94] Dispossession has been further entrenched by judicial interpretation of the Act's definition of native title. In essence, section 223 defines native title as the rights and interests of Aboriginal and Torres Strait Islander people in relation to lands and waters held under their traditional laws and customs. Section 223 further requires that by those laws and customs the native title holders have a 'connection' with the lands or waters, and that, the rights and interests are recognised by the common law of Australia.

The High Court has interpreted the traditional laws and customs required by s. 223 as those that were in existence at the time that the British acquired sovereignty.[95] As a consequence of such onerous requirements, native title is likely to be beyond the reach of those whose ancestors experienced massacres, forced removals and the policies that gave rise to the Stolen Generations. In a reflective piece on the *Native Title Act 1993* (Cth) the barrister who led the historic *Mabo* litigation, Dr. Bryan Keon-Cohen, observed that many have experienced the legislation as 'a complex, excessively legalistic and mean-spirited regime'.[96] Native title claimants who endure the indignity of having their family histories probed by strangers, could scarcely disagree.

Today, Indigenous people are among the poorest Australians, vulnerable to contact with the criminal justice system and prone to ill health. This is despite the many David and Goliath battles fought by generations

[93] Garth Nettheim, 'Judicial Revolution or Cautious Correction? *Mabo v Queensland*' (1993) 16(1) *University of New South Wales Law Journal*, 1, 23.

[94] See the validation provisions and future act regime contained in Part Two of the *Native Title Act 1993* (Cth).

[95] *Members of the Yorta Yorta Aboriginal Community v Victoria* [2002] HCA 58 [86] per Gleeson CJ, Gummow and Hayne JJ.

[96] Bryan Keon-Cohen, 'From Euphoria to Extinguishment to Co-existence' (2017) 23 *James Cook University Law Review*, 9, 11.

for the right to equality. Tragically, such victories are now mere symbols of an ideal Australia in which egalitarianism is the norm, and racism is confined to the random acts of flawed individuals.

Racism Is Omnipresent

In common with the USA, racism in Australia is pervasive. The Goenpul scholar, Professor Aileen Moreton-Robinson argues that whiteness is culturally based.[97] The shared beliefs, behaviours and values of white people alone define what is normal and imbue all of Australia's institutions. Every waking moment Australians are bombarded with representations of whiteness in magazines, billboards and television.[98] Landmarks such as the Queen Victoria Building in Sydney's central business district pay homage to a distant monarchy, but there is scant acknowledgement of those who nurtured the land underneath bitumen and steel for thousands of years.

Although the nation sits upon Indigenous lands, Indigenous people have been largely erased from Australia's foundation story. According to this story, Australia was built through the efforts of resourceful and courageous settlers.[99] The various invasions that resulted in a significant loss of life are seldom acknowledged by way of memorials. Attempts to make even minor accommodations to Indigenous peoples' sensibilities, such as changing the date of Australia's national day to one that is inclusive, are routinely rejected by the nation's political leaders.[100]

Cunningham and Paradies have categorised racism as internalised, interpersonal and systemic.[101] Internalised racism refers to an acceptance

[97] Aileen Moreton-Robinson, 'Witnessing Whiteness in the Wake of Wik' (1998) 17(2) *Social Alternatives*, 11.

[98] Aileen Moreton-Robinson, 'Unmasking Whiteness: A Goori Jondal's look at Some Duggai Business' (1999) 6(1) *Queensland Review*, 1, 2.

[99] Bob Hodge and Vijay Mishra, *Dark Side of the Dream: Australian Literature and the Postcolonial Mind* (Allen & Unwin, 1991).

[100] Scott Morrison, 'This is Why We Celebrate Australia Day on January 26' *Sydney Morning Herald* (online, 25 January 2019), https://www.smh.com.au/national/scott-morrison-this-is-why-we-celebrate-australia-day-on-january-26-20190125-p50tn8.html.

[101] Joan Cunningham and Yin C. Paradies, 'Patterns and Correlates of Self-Reported Racial Discrimination Among Australian Aboriginal and Torres Strait Islander Adults, 2008–09: Analysis of National Survey Data' (2013) 12(47) *International Journal for Equity in Health*, 1, 2.

of beliefs revolving around the inferiority of one's own racial or ethnic group. Interpersonal racism encompasses personal interactions that propagate inequalities across racial or ethnic groups. Systemic or institutional racism includes policies, practices and processes that perpetuate disadvantages suffered by particular racial or ethnic communities. The vast majority of Indigenous people have endured at least one of the three categories, and for many, racism is a burden carried throughout their daily lives.

Over a decade ago, Mellor conducted interviews with 34 Aboriginal people concerning their experiences of racism.[102] Mellor argued that victims' perspectives had been largely overlooked by prior research,[103] leading to an incomplete picture of the role of race in contemporary Australian society. The major conclusion from the study was that racism was a frequent, perhaps even daily experience:

> It constitutes a coherent complex of different kinds of verbal and physical behaviours, discrimination, and cultural domination and rejection that are experienced in diverse situations. In effect, these situations encompass all those that constitute everyday life: school, sport, shops, employment, public places, hotels, entertainment venues, transport, traffic, accommodation, and the socio/political environment. The racism is experienced to be present everywhere in society...[104]

Together with overt acts and subtle gestures, racism also manifests in gross indifference. On any marker, Indigenous people are among the most marginalised in Australian society, but their disadvantage in the criminal justice system is especially stark. Although Indigenous people comprise only three per cent of Australia's population, they account for just over a quarter of the nation's prison population.[105] Indigenous youth are a staggering 25 times more likely than other young Australians

[102] David Mellor, 'Contemporary Racism in Australia: The Experiences of Aborigines' (2003) 29(4) *Personality and Social Psychology Bulletin*, 474.

[103] Ibid., 482.

[104] Ibid., 483.

[105] Australian Institute of Health and Welfare, 'Australia's Welfare 2017: In Brief' (19 October 2017), https://www.aihw.gov.au/reports/australias-welfare/australias-welfare-2017-in-brief/contents/indigenous-australians.

to be incarcerated.[106] Yet the over-representation of Indigenous people in the criminal justice system is rarely a priority for Australia's political leadership.

No amount of upward mobility will protect an individual from racism. Entry into a prestigious profession, for example, does not spare one from the pain of bigotry. In a recent survey of its members by the Australian Indigenous Doctors Association, more than sixty per cent of respondents reported experiencing racism and or bullying almost every day, or at least once a week.[107] More than half reported negative reactions from colleagues in relation to their Indigenous heritage, which included perceptions of privileges and 'easier pathways' into medicine.[108] Not even fame can insulate an individual from racism. Adam Goodes may have scaled the heights of sporting success as one of the faces of the Australian Football League, but that did not protect him from racial slurs.[109]

In summary, the conditions that gave rise to the emergence of CRT in the USA find resonance in Australia. Since the beginning of colonisation, Australian society has been structured on racial lines. Advancements for Indigenous people have largely consisted of peaks of progress, which arrived at the tail end of gruelling campaigns. Just as Derrick Bell and his contemporaries watched the gains of civil rights victories dissipate over time, Indigenous people are left to wonder whatever became of the promise of triumphs such as the 1967 referendum and the *Mabo* decision.

Part Four: Australian CRT Scholarship

Introduction

In common with the founders of CRT, scholars in Australia have created new approaches to illuminate the ubiquity of racism. This part will introduce the work of two scholars who have built strong foundations for an Australian variation of CRT—Distinguished Professor Aileen

[106] Wayne Martin, 'Unequal Justice for Indigenous Australians' (2018) 14 *The Judicial Review*, 35.

[107] Australian Indigenous Doctors Association, *Report on the Findings of the 2016 AIDA Member Survey on Bullying, Racism and Lateral Violence in the Workplace* (2017), 10.

[108] Ibid., 6.

[109] Glenn D'Cruz, 'Breaking Bad: The Booing of Adam Goodes and the Politics of the Black Sports Celebrity in Australia' (2018) 9(1) *Celebrity Studies*, 131.

Moreton-Robinson and Dr. Debbie Bargallie. It will then acknowledge the contributions of legal scholars who are incorporating CRT into their work.

The Pioneers of Australian CRT

The leading proponent of Australian CRT is the Goenpul scholar, Distinguished Professor Aileen Moreton-Robinson. Twenty years ago, Professor Moreton-Robinson issued a challenge to Australian feminists to acknowledge their complicity in the colonial project when she wrote the book, *Talkin' Up to the White Woman.*[110] Professor Moreton-Robinson reasoned that by ignoring issues of race, feminist scholars had rendered their own racial privilege invisible.[111] Notions of a universal woman were also damaging to women from marginalised communities because the universal woman invariably reflected only the values and priorities of white middle-class women.

Much like CRT recognises that people of colour have a unique voice, Professor Moreton-Robinson argued that Indigenous women write from a distinct standpoint:

> An Indigenous woman's standpoint is shaped by the following themes. They include sharing an inalienable connection to land; a legacy of dispossession, racism and sexism; resisting and replacing disparaging images of ourselves with self-defined images; continuing our activism as mothers, sisters, aunts, daughters, grandmothers and community leaders, as well as negotiating sexual politics across and within cultures.[112]

Indigenous women defy white hegemony through means that include self-presentation. In their memoirs, often referred to as 'life stories', Indigenous women bring themselves and their communities to the centre. When Indigenous women write from their own, unique standpoint, they reveal not only multiple acts of defiance against subjugation, but also

[110] Aileen Moreton-Robinson, *Talkin' Up to the White Woman* (University of Queensland Press, 2000).

[111] Ibid., 33.

[112] Ibid., xvi.

complicity by white women in their domination.[113] Professor Moreton-Robinson concluded by appealing to feminist scholars to theorise and ultimately relinquish the privilege conferred by whiteness. Until this challenge was accepted, Indigenous women would continue to offer resistance by way of 'talkin' up', as 'the invisibility of unspeakable things requires them to be spoken'.[114]

Much of Professor Moreton-Robinson's subsequent work has interrogated patriarchal whiteness, which she describes as 'an invisible unnamed organizing principle that surreptitiously shapes social relations and economic development'.[115] In common with the CRT scholar, Cheryl Harris, Professor Moreton-Robinson argues that patriarchal whiteness is a form of property that encompasses rights in relation to tangible objects and incorporeal assets such as reputation.[116] As distinct from white Australians, who were conferred proprietary rights from the earliest days of colonisation, Indigenous people have never enjoyed the privilege of being 'property-owning' subjects.[117] Even the belated recognition of native title is a pyrrhic victory because the rights that comprise native title are often inferior to other forms of proprietary rights, and are vulnerable to extinguishment.

Like American CRT scholars, Professor Moreton-Robinson is critical of 'color-blindness'.[118] The myth that Australia is the 'land of the fair go' erases the inherited wealth of those whose ancestors profited from the theft of Indigenous lands. It also renders invisible the myriad dimensions of racial privilege, that include, 'not having to educate white children about systemic racism for their protection and having white identity affirmed in society on a daily basis through positive representations in the media, government policies, legislation, and the education system'.[119]

More recently, the Kamilaroi and Wonnarua scholar, Dr. Debbie Bargallie extended the work of Professor Moreton-Robinson when she

[113] Ibid., 10.

[114] Ibid., 186.

[115] Aileen Moreton-Robinson, *The White Possessive: Property, Power, and Indigenous Sovereignty* (University of Minnesota Press, 2015), 66.

[116] Ibid.

[117] Ibid., 93.

[118] Ibid., 96.

[119] Ibid., 97.

cast a CRT lens over the experiences of Indigenous employees in the Australian Public Service ('APS'). Dr. Bargallie's analysis was published in the book, *Unmasking the Racial Contract*.[120] Dr. Bargallie's research was inspired by her own experience of almost fourteen years of employment in the APS.[121] During that time Dr. Bargallie frequently encountered racist remarks and was denied advantages enjoyed by her non-Indigenous colleagues, which included opportunities for career advancement. She described her experiences as being killed 'softly' and having her 'spirit broken'.[122] Although she was patently aware that racism was a common occurrence in the APS, those within senior management operated as though it did not exist.

Dr. Bargallie drew upon aspects of CRT, namely everyday racism, microaggressions and racial contract theory. The latter was conceived by the Jamaican scholar, Professor Charles W. Mills to describe a series of formal and informal agreements, whose purpose is 'always the differential privileging of whites as a group with respect to the nonwhites as a group'.[123] Dr. Bargallie argues that in Australia, the racial contract began with invasion and the beginning of colonisation.[124] It has mutated over time, and in its current guise the racial contract propagates a façade of equality.[125]

In contemporary workplaces, the racial contract is reinforced by microaggressions, that is, the commonplace and often subtle slights that are designed to keep members of racialised communities in 'their place'.[126] Through her conversations with Indigenous public servants, Dr. Bargallie exposed a 'taxonomy' of microaggressions, which included

[120] Debbie Bargallie, *Unmasking the Racial Contract: Indigenous Voices on Racism in the Australian Public Service* (Aboriginal Studies Press, 2020)

[121] Ibid., 33.

[122] Ibid., 42.

[123] Charles W. Mills, *The Racial Contract* (Cornell University Press, 1997), 11.

[124] Bargallie (n 120), 92.

[125] Ibid.

[126] Ibid., 96.

hyper-surveillance and the normalization of racist language.[127] Indigenous public servants also had to contend with assumptions that they lacked intelligence and were unable to write to the 'expected standard'.[128]

Australian legal scholars began to use CRT to cast light on the nexus between law and race in the early 2000s. For example, Janet Ramsley and Elena Marchetti applied whiteness theory to the judgment of O'Loughlin J. in *Cubillo and Gunner v Commonwealth*.[129] Lorna Cubillo and Peter Gunner were members of the Stolen Generations, who pursued legal action against the Commonwealth in respect of harms they suffered after being removed from their families. Ultimately, their attempt to achieve legal redress was unsuccessful. In their analysis of the judgment, Ramsely and Marchetti revealed various assumptions that affirmed the dominance of whiteness while causing detriment to the plaintiffs, such as a preference for documentary evidence over oral testimony.[130]

It was also in the early 2000s that Indigenous legal scholars gained a foothold in Australian law schools. The Tanganekald and Meintangk scholar, Professor Irene Watson, blazed a trail when she created space for Indigenous voices in Australia's law journals. Professor Watson warned Indigenous people against placing their faith in constructs such as native title, which deflected from the crucial imperatives of caring for the land and restoring Indigenous people's own time-honoured laws.[131] When writing about their experiences of working in law schools, some Indigenous scholars incorporated the principles of CRT in their scholarship. For example, the Nyungar woman, Dr. Hannah McGlade, drew upon CRT in her reflective piece on being an associate lecturer at her alma mater, the University of Western Australia.[132]

127 Ibid., 105–110.

128 Ibid., 105.

129 *Cubillo and Gunner v Commonwealth* (2000) 174 ALR 97. Janet Ramsley and Elena Marchetti, 'The Hidden Whiteness of Australian Law: A Case Study' (2001) 10 *Griffith Law Review*, 139.

130 Ibid., 146.

131 Irene Watson, 'Power of the Muldarbi, the Road to its Demise' (1998) 11 *Australian Feminist Law Journal*, 28.

132 Hannah McGlade, 'The Day of the Minstrel Show' (2005) 6(8) *Indigenous Law Bulletin*, 16. See also Nicole Watson, 'Indigenous People in Legal Education: Staring into a Mirror Without Reflection' (2005) 6(8) *Indigenous Law Bulletin*, 4.

Later, the Gomeroi-Kamilaroi scholar, Marcelle Burns and Jennifer Nielsen interrogated the absence of race from legal curricula, which resulted in the attribution of race to the Other, and the invisibility of whiteness as a 'position of power'.[133] More recently, scholars have begun to cast a CRT lens over laws and policies that disproportionately impact upon Indigenous people and members of other marginalised communities.[134]

Conclusion

Critical race theory emerged out of recognition that despite the achievements of those who fought in the trenches of the civil rights movement, racism continued to be a virulent and unrelenting force that permeated American society. Founders such as Derrick Bell recognised that racism was not only omnipresent, it was also permanent. Proponents of CRT counter the racial hierarchy with the narratives of those who sit on its bottom rung. By giving voice to those within marginalised communities, CRT scholars challenge dominant mindsets, empower those who have been dehumanised by the various manifestations of racism, and challenge their audience to believe that a better world is possible.

Critical race feminism has much in common with CRT, such as the use of storytelling as methodology. However, CRF scholars bring the voices of women of colour to the centre of their analysis. They have also created intellectual tools, such as intersectionality, which recognises that aspects of a person's identity such as race, gender and sexuality coincide and lead to specific kinds of discrimination.

This chapter has argued that CRT should be extended to Australia out of recognition of three commonalities with the USA. Firstly, since the beginning of colonisation, Australian society has been structured on racial lines. Secondly, any gains that Indigenous people have made have been preceded by long and strenuous campaigns. Over time, however,

[133] Marcelle Burns and Jennifer Nielsen 'Dealing with the "Wicked" Problem of Race and the Law: A Critical Journey for Students (and Academics)' (2018) 28 *Legal Education Review*, 1, 2.

[134] Shelley Bielefeld and Fleur Beaupert, 'Income Management and Intersectionality: Analysing Compulsory Income Management Through the Lenses of Critical Race Theory and Disability Studies ('Discrit')' (2019) 41(3) *Sydney Law Review*, 327. See also Alison Whittaker, 'One-Punch Drunk: White Masculinities as a Property Right in New South Wales' Assault Causing Death Law Reforms' (2020) *Australian Feminist Law Journal*, 1.

those victories have lost momentum. Finally, racism in Australia is ever-present, and for many Indigenous people, racism is a burden that is carried throughout their daily lives.

In recent decades, scholars have begun to extend CRT to illuminate Australia's racial hierarchy and identify the myriad ways that it cements the disadvantaged position of Indigenous people. The foundations for this intellectual movement were built by the likes of Professor Aileen Moreton-Robinson, who has interrogated various aspects of patriarchal whiteness. More recently, Dr. Debbie Bargallie cast a CRT lens over the experiences of Indigenous employees of the APS. Legal scholars have also begun to incorporate CRT into their work to expose how racism is embedded in legal education, judicial decision making and legislation.

CHAPTER 3

Outlaw Women: Emerging from Invisibility to Resistance

Abstract This chapter begins by considering the relationship between degrading representations of Indigenous women and colonisation. Such representations not only deprived Indigenous women of voice, but they also provided an alibi for the systematic abuse of Indigenous women by settler men. The chapter will then provide a glimpse into the history of Indigenous women's outlaw culture. Finally, the chapter will discuss the treatment of Indigenous women in legal storytelling. It will conclude by arguing in favour of using speculative biography as a device to imagine the stories of Indigenous women who appear in judgments, so that their agency and ingenuity are brought to light.

Keywords Indigenous women · Representations · Outlaw culture

Introduction

Indigenous women have an extraordinary record of contributing to public life. Among the stalwarts of the struggle for Indigenous rights was Oodgeroo Noonuccal of the Noonuccal People of Minjerribah, also known as Kath Walker. She would become the first Indigenous

N. Watson, *Aboriginal Women, Law and Critical Race Theory*, Palgrave Studies in Race, Ethnicity, Indigeneity and Criminal Justice, https://doi.org/10.1007/978-3-030-87327-1_3

person to publish a book of poems,[1] and was at the vanguard of the campaign to remove racially discriminatory provisions from the *Constitution*.[2] Oodgeroo Noonuccal was but one of many Indigenous women who were unwavering in their commitment to improve the lives of the most marginalised members of their communities. Sadly, however, Indigenous women are seldom acknowledged for their contributions.

At the same time, Indigenous women have been harmed by colonial myths that painted them as promiscuous and brutish. Such mythology provided an alibi for the rampant abuse of Indigenous women by settler men, while depriving victims of the protection of the law. In response, generations of Indigenous women created practices and tactics that fall within the domain of outlaw culture. Outlaw culture has found expression both outside of the parameters of the law and through compliance with the law. Black outlaw women became bushrangers, strikers and absconders. Others strove to create a sanctuary for vulnerable people, and on occasion, used the law as a tool of empowerment.

This chapter will be divided into three parts. Part one will discuss the relationship between colonisation and popular representations of Indigenous women. In part two I will argue that akin to the African American experience, Indigenous women have been at the cutting edge of an outlaw culture. Examples of outlaw culture are buried in historical accounts, memoirs and testimony to inquiries. Finally, part three will explore the portrayals of Indigenous women in legal storytelling. All too often, the narratives of Indigenous women are absent from judgments. I will argue that by contextualising judgments with socio-legal materials, the stories of Indigenous women can be reimagined to recognise their agency and resilience.

[1] Oodgeroo Noonuccal, *We are Going: Poems* (Jacaranda Press, 1966).

[2] Karen Fox, 'Oodgeroo Noonuccal: Media Snapshots of a Controversial Life' in Peter Read, Frances Peters-Little and Anna Haebich (eds), *Indigenous Biography and Autobiography* (ANU Press, 2008), 57.

Part One: Popular Representations of Indigenous Women

Introduction

In her book, *Finding Eliza: Power and Colonial Storytelling*[3] the Eualeyai/Kamillaroi scholar, Larissa Behrendt illuminated the relationship between the brutal dispossession of Indigenous people and colonial narratives epitomised by the Eliza Fraser legend. Together with her husband, Captain James Fraser, Eliza was aboard the ship, Stirling Castle when its hull was torn apart during a violent storm in May 1836.[4] The survivors drifted near the east coast of Australia. Several weeks later they disembarked on the beautiful lands of the Butchulla people, which would later be named after Captain Fraser.

Soon after their arrival, the hapless Captain perished. The Butchulla cared for Eliza for almost two months until she was rescued.[5] Upon her return to colonial society, Eliza garnered public sympathy with embellished accounts of the Butchulla. While portraying all of the Butchulla as vicious, Eliza was particularly scathing of the women. According to Behrendt, the Black women who featured in Eliza's story were, 'worse in their conduct, uglier in their appearance and more lacking in compassion for her than the men'.[6]

Eliza's narrative was at odds with Butchulla oral histories. According to which, it was the women who tended to her painful sunburn and marked her body with white ochre, to notify others that Eliza had been given the sanctuary of their camp.[7] Instead of acknowledging the efforts of those who saved her life, Eliza repaid them with self-serving falsehoods. The Eliza Fraser legend provides an opening to the themes unpacked by this part. Colonial myths denied Indigenous women their voices while portraying them as barbarous. Such representations belonged to a system of ideas that concealed unpalatable truths about Australia's beginnings.

[3] Larissa Behrendt, *Finding Eliza: Power and Colonial Storytelling* (University of Queensland Press, 2016).

[4] Ibid., 11.

[5] Ibid., 30.

[6] Ibid., 23.

[7] Ibid., 58–59.

Indigenous Women in Australian History

Hodge and Mishra argue that representations of Indigenous people have always played a crucial role in the maintenance of Australia's foundation myth,[8] that is, the narrative that Australia was built by brave and resourceful white settlers. To uphold the foundation myth Indigenous people were largely erased, but not entirely. Demeaning representations of Indigenous people were useful because they obscured the reality that Australia was founded upon an unjust invasion.[9]

For the most part, Indigenous women have been absent from Australian history. Those who were recognised were invariably portrayed in ways that served the interests of settlers. The most prominent Indigenous woman in Australian history, Truganini was variously cast as an Australian version of Pocahontas, an esteemed Indigenous member of the British Empire and the last survivor of a vanquished race.[10] Missing from such portrayals was the voice of Truganini herself.

Born in the early nineteenth century to the Nuenonne clan in what is now known as Tasmania, Truganini's life was characterised by profound loss.[11] As a child she saw her mother murdered by sailors,[12] and her sisters kidnapped by sealers.[13] The man she had planned to marry would also be brutally killed by sawyers.[14] When 16 or 17 years old, Truganini met George Augustus Robinson,[15] who would be charged with achieving a conciliation between the settlers and Indigenous people who survived the carnage of the British invasion. Truganini would accompany Robinson on his missions and on at least one occasion she saved his life.[16]

[8] Bob Hodge and Vijay Mishra, *Dark Side of the Dream: Australian Literature and the Postcolonial Mind* (Allen & Unwin, 1991).

[9] Ibid., 26.

[10] Karen Fox, *Maori and Aboriginal Women in the Public Eye: Representing Difference, 1950–2000* (ANU Press, 2011), 4.

[11] Cassandra Pybus, *Truganini: Journey Through the Apocalypse* (Allen & Unwin, 2020), xv.

[12] Ibid., 8.

[13] Ibid., 9.

[14] Lyndall Ryan, *Tasmanian Aborigines: A History since 1803* (Allen & Unwin, 2012), 268.

[15] Pybus (n 11), 12.

[16] Ryan (n 14), 268.

Two years after her death in 1867, Truganini's remains were exhumed at the behest of the Royal Society of Tasmania, which considered her to be nothing more than an object to be studied.[17] This denial of Truganini's humanity was exemplified by the now notorious advocate of eugenics and professor of anatomy, Richard Berry[18] who explained her passing as proof of 'the failure of an inferior race to thrive in the presence of a civilized people.'[19] It would not be until a century after her death that Truganini's remains were finally returned to her countrymen, who scattered her ashes in the D'Entrecasteaux Channel.[20]

In her book, *Skin Deep: Settler Impressions of Aboriginal Women*[21] Liz Conor unpacked the various tropes through which the settlers came to know Indigenous women. Among the tropes examined by Conor was 'bride capture',[22] that is, the representation of Indigenous women as the wretched victims of Black male savagery. Conor traced this trope back to David Collins, the Lieutenant-Governor and Deputy Judge Advocate of the Colony of New South Wales.[23] When writing about his new surroundings, Collins relayed the brutal kidnapping of an Indigenous woman. Although he did not witness the kidnapping, Collins vividly described the victim being 'stupefied with blows' before being 'dragged through the woods by one arm, with a perseverance and violence that one might suppose would displace it from its socket'.[24] This account was subsequently used by others to demonstrate the apparent barbarity inherent in all unions between Indigenous men and women. The trope of bride capture affirmed that all Indigenous people were on the 'bottom rung of the ladder of race destiny'.[25] It also enabled men such as Collins

[17] Ibid., 270.

[18] Ross L. Jones, 'Eugenics in Australia: The Secret of Melbourne's Elite', *The Conversation*, 21 September 2011, https://theconversation.com/eugenics-in-australia-the-secret-of-melbournes-elite-3350.

[19] Ryan (n 14), 270.

[20] Fox (n 10), 4.

[21] Liz Conor, *Skin Deep: Settler Impressions of Aboriginal Women* (UWA Press, 2016).

[22] Ibid., 90–151.

[23] Liz Conor, 'It's Time to Remove the Offenders' *ABC News* (Opinion Piece, 8 March 2012), https://www.abc.net.au/news/2012-03-08/conor-it27s-time-to-remove-the-offenders/3875014.

[24] Conor (n 21), 103.

[25] Ibid., 116.

to view colonisation as an exercise in chivalry. Rather than being complicit in the dispossession of Indigenous people, they were bringing the benefits of 'civilisation' to an inferior race.

Indigenous women were also maligned for their alleged promiscuity. According to Conor, Black female sexuality was seen as both a 'frontier resource' and a 'necessary evil' in parts of the country where there were few white women.[26] Suggestions of ill-treatment of Black women were often met with claims that the alleged victims were lacking in morals. In one example cited by Conor, men who were accused of abducting Aboriginal women were defended by the pastoralist, Alfred Giles, who claimed that the notion of 'chastity' among Indigenous women was 'preposterous'.[27]

A related trope debased Indigenous mothers by painting them as avid practitioners of infanticide.[28] Among the most ardent proponents of this falsehood was the journalist, Daisy Bates. Bates made the venal claim that Indigenous mothers practiced cannibalism on their own children in newspaper articles published in the 1920s[29] and her bestselling book, *The Passing of the Aborigines*.[30] After her death in 1951, Bates' fabrications continued to have some lingering influence. In the 1990s the One Nation senator, Pauline Hanson deferred to Bates' work in her assaults on Indigenous people.[31]

Enmeshed in the imagery of the jezebel, the Black man's chattel and the ferocious mother were offensive terms such as 'Gin' and 'lubra'. The first settlers to use the latter interpreted it to mean 'wife'.[32] Over time,

[26] Liz Conor, '"Black Velvet" and "Purple Indignation": Print Responses to Japanese "poaching" of Aboriginal Women" (2013) 37 *Aboriginal History*, 51, 55.

[27] Ibid., 57.

[28] Conor (n 21), 152–238.

[29] Lisa Waller, 'Singular Influence: Mapping the Ascent of Daisy M. Bates in Popular Understanding and Indigenous Policy' (2010) 37(2) *Australian Journal of Communication*, 1, 8.

[30] Daisy Bates, *The Passing of the Aborigines: A Lifetime Spent Among the Natives of Australia* (Murray, 1938).

[31] L. R. Hiatt, *The Rise and Fall of Daisy O'Dwyer* (2006) 2 *Australian Aboriginal Studies*, 111, 112.

[32] Liz Conor, 'The "Lubra" Type in Australian Imaginings of the Aboriginal Woman from 1836–1973' (2013) 25(2) *Gender & History*, 230, 233.

it would come to symbolise lax sexual mores and racial differences.[33] Such terminology was normalised and resounded in popular culture. In his analysis of stigmatising trademarks,[34] Fady Aoun identified early Australian trademarks that are nauseating in their portrayals of Indigenous women. Among them was 'Lubra Boot Polish' which transposed ape-like characteristics onto the face of an Indigenous woman,[35] and 'A Dry Gin'[36] which featured an emaciated Black woman sitting on a log. In a reference to the annual distribution of blankets to impoverished Indigenous people, her naked body was adorned with a blanket.[37]

Contemporary appropriations of Black women are less confronting, but they continue to be problematic. I am reminded of this often as I cross the Sydney Harbour Bridge to go to work. South of the bridge is Sydney's most vibrant waterfront precinct, Barangaroo. For those who can afford it, there is luxurious accommodation at Crown Towers Sydney, which at 275 metres high, is the city's tallest hotel.[38] Residential apartments can also be purchased in the complex, One Barangaroo with some apartments selling for millions of dollars.[39] Yet to open its doors is the lavish Barangaroo Casino,[40] which has been mired in controversy since an inquiry revealed that its owner, Crown Resorts was complicit in money laundering.

Supporters of the development have highlighted the public benefits of the nearby Barangaroo Reserve. What was previously Sydney's oldest

[33] Ibid., 236.

[34] Fady J. G. Aoun, 'Whitewashing Australia's History of Stigmatising Trade Marks and Commercial Imagery' (2019) 42(3) *Melbourne University Law Review*, 671.

[35] Ibid., 703.

[36] Ibid., 691.

[37] Ibid., 692.

[38] Craig Platt, 'Crown Towers Hotel opens at Crown Sydney, Barangaroo' *Traveller* (online, 28 December 2020), https://www.traveller.com.au/crown-towers-hotel-opens-at-crown-sydney-barangaroo-h1t2f9.

[39] Jonathan Chancellor, 'Mega-Wealthy Buyers Move into Crown Casino's One Barangaroo Tower', *The Daily Telegraph* (online, 19 April 2021), https://www.realestate.com.au/news/megawealthy-buyers-move-into-crown-casinos-one-barangaroo-tower/.

[40] Josh Bavas, 'The Damning Evidence That Brought Crown Resorts to its Knees' *ABC News* (online, 25 October 2020), https://www.abc.net.au/news/2020-10-25/inquiry-evidence-that-brought-crown-resorts-to-its-knees/12806694.

industrial site has been transformed into parklands.[41] My partner and I have meandered through the Barangaroo Reserve on the occasional, lazy Saturday afternoon. It offers a majestic view of one of the world's most picturesque harbours. But I cringe when my mind turns to the Black woman who is its namesake.

Barangaroo was a Cammeraygal woman and wife of one of the most tragic figures in Australian history, Bennelong. The ambitious warrior would form a complex relationship with the first Governor of the Colony of New South Wales, Arthur Phillip. Barangaroo was known for her strident independence, charisma and outspokenness.[42] Upon witnessing a convict being flogged, Barangaroo is reported to have 'seized a stick, and made to wallop the flogger'.[43] Unlike her husband who had a flair for the colonisers' clothing, Barangaroo refused to assume their customs.[44] All of which begs the question—how would the real Barangaroo feel about her name becoming synonymous with extravagance outside of the grasp of all but a privileged few?

Part Two: Indigenous Women's Outlaw Culture

Introduction

My life changed indelibly when my father died suddenly in late 2019. During that painful time, my family was able to draw comfort from traditions that are felt more than named. As news broke of his passing, we became enveloped in the love of so many whose lives had been touched by my father. I was humbled by my father's old friends from the turbulent days of the Tent Embassy,[45] who travelled during catastrophic fires

[41] 'Barangaroo Reserve Opens to the Public' *Sydney Morning Herald* (Sydney, 20 August 2015), https://www.smh.com.au/national/nsw/barangaroo-reserve-opens-to-the-public-20150820-gj3ekl.html.

[42] Inga Clendinnen, *Dancing with Strangers: Europeans and Australians at First Contact* (Cambridge University Press, 2005), 201–213.

[43] Ibid., 176.

[44] Ibid., 207.

[45] The Tent Embassy was established by young activists on the lawns of the Australian Parliament in 1972, in response to the Australia Day Statement made by the former Prime Minister, William McMahon, in which he declined to support Aboriginal land rights. See Gary Foley, Andrew Schaap and Edwina Howell (eds), *The Aboriginal Tent Embassy: Sovereignty, Black Power, Land Rights and the State* (Routledge, 2013).

to bid him farewell. The anecdotes about Dad that we shared over gentle laughter were balms to my aching soul.

Indigenous people have many traditions, more often lived rather than articulated, which provide an anchor during times of adversity. This part is about those that fall under the umbrella of Indigenous women's outlaw culture. Generations of Black women have been compelled to create a stratagem of tactics and practices to provide sanctuary from the violence of colonisation. In common with the outlaw culture articulated by Monica Evans,[46] Indigenous women's outlaw culture is manifest in a spectrum of relationships with the law.

Because of the invisibility of Indigenous women, their outlaw culture has been overlooked by scholars. However, examples of outlaw culture can be gleaned from historical texts, memoirs, oral histories and testimony to inquiries. The following part will draw upon such resources to piece together a historical snapshot of two dimensions of Indigenous women's outlaw culture—removing one's self outside of the law and operating within the parameters of the law to protect the most vulnerable members of the community. In such a brief piece, it is impossible to acknowledge even a minute fraction of all the women who exercised autonomy in the face of unremitting subjugation. However, by writing this book I hope that other scholars will be prompted to engage with these important stories.

Operating Outside of the Law

It is difficult to imagine the terror instilled in the women who watched their homes, families, indeed everything that had defined their worlds, devastated by invasion. As British subjects, Indigenous women were entitled to the protection of the rule of law. In reality, that counted for little. On the frontier the Native Police and settlers kidnapped, raped and murdered Indigenous women with impunity. Despite everything, some women empowered themselves by breaking the law.

The names of those who took up arms are unknown to most Australians. A rare exception is the Palawa warrior, Tarenorerer or Walyer, who was born in what was then known as the Colony of Van Diemen's

[46] Monica J. Evans, 'Stealing Away: Black Women, Outlaw Culture and the Rhetoric of Rights' (1993) 28 *Harvard Civil Rights—Civil Liberties Law Review*, 263.

Land in the early nineteenth century.[47] As a young woman, Walyer was sold to sealers in exchange for dogs and flour.[48] After escaping her captors in 1828, Walyer taught members of her clan how to use firearms and led their resistance against the settlers.[49] Walyer became notorious for hurling insults at her enemies during attacks, and reportedly said that she liked the White men 'as she did a black snake'.[50] Walyer's brief but momentous life ended after she contracted influenza in May 1831.[51]

Other outlaw women secured a degree of autonomy by forging partnerships with male bushrangers. Among them was Mary Cockerill, who was born in Van Diemen's Land in the late eighteenth century.[52] Mary met the Island's most notorious bushranger, Michael Howe when she was still a child. According to the historian, Kay Saunders they eloped in either late 1814 or early 1815.[53] Mary would go on to become an 'armed and active bushranger,'[54] participating in raids on hapless settlers.

Decades later the Worimi woman, Mary Ann Bugg formed a relationship with Frederick Wordsworth Ward, who would become known as 'Captain Thunderbolt'. Mary Ann was born near Gloucester, New South Wales in 1834.[55] It is uncertain when Mary Ann met Ward, but we do know that she gave birth to their first child in October 1861.[56] For some time before their union came to an end in 1867, Mary Ann was Ward's 'chief lieutenant and right-hand man'.[57] Mary Ann not only rode alongside Ward. It is believed that she also helped him to overcome illiteracy, and on occasion, deliberately spread misinformation about

[47] Ryan (n 14), 172.

[48] Ibid.

[49] Kay Saunders, *Notorious Australian Women* (HarperCollins, 2011), 37.

[50] Vicki maikutena Matson-Green, 'Tarenorerer (1800–1831)' *Australian Dictionary of Biography*, https://adb.anu.edu.au/biography/tarenorerer-13212.

[51] Ryan (n 14), 182.

[52] Saunders (n 49), 25.

[53] Ibid., 26.

[54] Ibid., 29.

[55] David Andrew Roberts and Carol Baxter, '"Mrs Thunderbolt": Setting the Record Straight on the Life and Times of Mary Ann Bugg' (2013) 99(1) *Journal of the Royal Australian Historical Society*, 55.

[56] Ibid., 57.

[57] Ibid., 55 citing the *Maitland Mercury*.

his whereabouts.[58] Stories handed down by generations of Indigenous families suggest that women who entered relationships with bushrangers were crucial to the men's success in evading the authorities. According to Kamilaroi oral histories,[59] women such as Mary Ann not only shared their knowledge of Country with their partners, but they also incorporated the men into their family relationships. The 'bush telegraph' armed the likes of Ward with valuable information about police movements.[60]

Later outlaw women found sanctuary by fleeing from the authorities and drawing upon their shrewdness and experiential knowledge to survive. This aspect of outlaw culture was personified by Molly and Daisy Craig and their cousin, Gracie Fields whose story would be memorialised by Doris Pilkington's book, *Follow the Rabbit-Proof Fence*,[61] which would later be turned into an award-winning film by Phillip Noyce.[62] The three children were removed from their families in Jigalong in the north-west of Western Australia in 1931. Their inconsolable relatives were informed by a police officer that the girls would be sent hundreds of miles away to the Moore River Native Settlement to receive an education.[63] On arrival, the children realised that the Settlement was more of a penitentiary than a school. They were forced to live in a crowded dormitory with iron bars on the windows, and those who attempted to flee were liable to receive cruel punishments that included solitary confinement.[64]

Unsurprisingly, Molly, Daisy and Gracie resolved to escape. Molly, whose father had worked as an inspector on a rabbit-proof fence that traversed Western Australia, knew that it would take them back to Jigalong.[65] After fleeing from the Settlement, the children began their 1600-

[58] Michael Dulaney, 'Mary Ann Bugg, the Aboriginal Bushranger Erased from Australian Folklore' *ABC News* (online, 17 November 2019), https://www.abc.net.au/news/2019-11-17/mary-ann-bugg-bushranger-partner-captain-thunderbolt/11699992.

[59] Kali Bierens, 'The Captain's Lady: Mary Ann Bugg' (Bachelor of Arts Honours Thesis, University of Tasmania, 2008), 22–23.

[60] Ibid., 22.

[61] Doris Pilkington, *Follow the Rabbit-Proof Fence* (University of Queensland Press, 2nd ed, 2002).

[62] *Rabbit-Proof Fence* (Rumbalara Films, 2002).

[63] Pilkington (n 61), 44.

[64] Ibid., 64–71.

[65] Ibid., 78.

kilometre trek home,[66] which would span over almost nine weeks.[67] During their long and perilous journey, the children survived by hunting rabbits and other small animals, and seeking food from farmhouses. They also gave false information to the adults whom they met to 'foil their would-be-captors'.[68]

Rather than return home, some outlaw women reclaimed their autonomy by moving outside of the purview of the authorities. When the Senate Standing Committee on Legal and Constitutional Affairs examined the lasting impacts of state control over the wages of Indigenous workers, it heard evidence from one woman who 'ran away' from a life of demeaning regulation:

> I ran away ... in 1967, just two days after my father's funeral. I borrowed $12 from my married sister rather than go to the police station and be interrogated about what I wanted my money for. Growing up, that is all you saw – our people, my parents, my sisters and other family members being questioned: 'What do you want your money for? You don't have any money'. It was humiliating and degrading. So I left, a 16 1/2-year-old, and started a new life in Townsville. That $12 was the best investment I have ever made. I educated myself.[69]

Other outlaw women resisted oppressive working conditions by going on strike. Among them were the domestic servants who participated in the historic Pilbara Strike. On 1 May 1946, hundreds of Aboriginal pastoral workers in the Pilbara abandoned their employment and demanded a fair wage.[70] Denied the protection of state and federal awards, Black workers commonly received paltry earnings, and in some instances only rations.[71] Despite police harassment and the ever-looming threat of imprisonment,

[66] Tony Birch, '"This is a True Story": Rabbit-Proof Fence, "Mr Devil" and the Desire to Forget' (2002) 8(1) *Cultural Studies Review*, 117.

[67] Pilkington (n 61), 130.

[68] Ibid., 100.

[69] Evidence to the Standing Committee on Legal and Constitutional Affairs, The Senate, Brisbane, 25 October 2006 [5.27] (Mrs Yvonne Butler).

[70] Julie Armstrong, 'On the Freedom Track to Narawunda: The Pilbara Aboriginal Pastoral Workers' Strike, 1946–1998' (2001) 22 *Studies in Western Australian History*, 23, 29.

[71] Ibid., 27.

the strikers persevered for years until employers finally agreed to make concessions.[72]

Victoria Haskins and Anne Scrimgeour argue that the participation of Black women domestic workers in the strike has been largely overlooked by historians.[73] Domestic workers commonly began their working day before sunrise and would tend to the cooking, cleaning and laundry for employer families.[74] Despite their important contributions to station life, domestic workers were denied wages and often forced to live in abominable conditions. According to one who joined the strike, domestic workers were fed substandard food, and forced to eat in a woodheap without so much as a plate for their meal.[75] When such women went on strike the impacts were keenly felt by their employers. Not only did white women have to tend to household chores, but the disappearance of servants also resulted in a loss of 'gentry' status for the entire family.[76]

The above-mentioned Senate Standing Committee on Legal and Constitutional Affairs also received evidence from Indigenous women in Queensland who risked incarceration and even permanent removal from their families, when they went on strike:

> I worked in the hospital ... The hours were long and our wages were £2 10s a fortnight. The staff who came there said, 'We're being paid big money, and youse are doing all the work'. You name it, we did it. We looked after patients and we scrubbed the floor. We got on our hands and knees, we scrubbed, we cleaned and we polished – you name it. And one day I organised about six of us: we went on strike for more wages. So we were marched down to the Superintendent's office and he said to us in no uncertain terms, 'I'll give you 24 hours to go back to work or I'll put you in jail'. If you spoke up for your rights, you were sent to jail for three

[72] Ibid., 33.

[73] Victoria Haskins and Anne Scrimgeour, '"Strike Strike, We Strike": Making Aboriginal Domestic Labor Visible in the Pilbara Pastoral Workers' Strike, Western Australia, 1946–1952' (2015) 88 *International Labor and Working-Class History*, 87.

[74] Ibid., 93.

[75] Ibid., 94.

[76] Ibid., 99.

weeks. Your only diet was black sweetened tea and bread and jam. If you continued to speak out you were sent to Palm Island, which was referred to as a punishment island.[77]

Caring for the Most Vulnerable

Operating outside of the boundary of law is just one tactic falling under the rubric of Black women's outlaw culture. Another is to create safety by remaining within the confines of the law and protecting the welfare of the most vulnerable. In common with the African American Clubwomen,[78] some Indigenous women realised that their individual rights and freedoms counted for little unless such gains were realised for all members of their communities. This often meant assuming responsibility for children within one's extended family, and children who were simply in need of love and care.

In her memoir,[79] Shirley Smith whose extraordinary life is discussed below, acknowledged the resourceful women who provided such care before the emergence of Indigenous community organisations in the 1970s. Often devout Christians and already raising children of their own, these women 'managed to squeeze a few pennies from somewhere'[80] to rear those in precarious circumstances. In her memoir, *Don't Take Your Love to Town*,[81] Ruby Langford Ginibi similarly acknowledged women such as her Aunt Nell. After her mother left their family and their father needed to work, nine-year-old Ruby and her siblings were sent to live with their Uncle Sam and Aunt Nell.[82] Seemingly without question, Aunt Nell and Uncle Sam raised the sisters as their own, leading Ruby to describe them as 'the best parents we could have had'.[83]

[77] Evidence to the Standing Committee on Legal and Constitutional Affairs, The Senate, Perth, 25 October 2006 [5.29] (Mrs Alexander Gater).

[78] Michelle Rief, 'Thinking Locally, Acting Globally: The International Agenda of African American Clubwomen, 1880–1940' (2004) 89(3) *The Journal of African American History*, 203.

[79] Shirley Smith and Bobbi Sykes, *MumShirl* (Heinemann Publishers, 1981).

[80] Ibid., 42.

[81] Ruby Langford Ginibi, *Don't Take Your Love to Town* (University of Queensland Press, 1988).

[82] Ibid., 9–10.

[83] Ibid., 10.

As I was reading Langford Ginibi's powerful book, I reflected on the matriarchs who played such an important role in my own childhood. They were women like my paternal grandmother, 'Nanna' with whom we lived for many years. It was under Nanna's influence that our home became a merry-go-round of uncles, aunts, cousins and restless souls who found an anchor in our family. Regardless of the number of people who lived in our house at any one time, Sunday dinners were often grand affairs, with roast meat and vegetables, followed by generous servings of bread-and-butter pudding. Nanna was never soft and she would often scold we children for speaking out of turn. But when I reminisce about my childhood, I feel grateful for the values that she imparted to us.

Few Indigenous women of Nanna's generation had the means to gain a formal education. Despite their limited opportunities, such women drew upon their experiential knowledge and resourcefulness to create spaces of sanctuary. One woman who personified this dimension of outlaw culture was Shirley Smith or MumShirl. While tending to her brother in prison, Smith was asked to call upon other inmates who were not receiving visitors. Soon male and female prisoners came to depend on her sympathetic ear.[84] At the same time, people outside of the prison system began to seek her counsel. In her memoir, Smith described a 'way of life' in which she used her empathy to create a safety net for those in need:

> My work, and the work of other Blacks who are doing things in a similar sort of way as I do, is very hard to talk about, probably because it is not a job, it is a way of life. We don't start at any particular time in our lives, or at any particular time of the day. If the door knocks in the middle of the night, we open it. If the phone rings, we answer it. Saturdays and Sundays run into each other. We can be up all night talking with some person who has that sort of problem, out at the prison at early morning, back at the Courts at 10 o'clock, at the Aboriginal Medical Service at mid-day, at the Children's Court in the afternoon, at a meeting to talk with some people about what we are doing in the evening, and likely as not, another meeting in the night.
>
> Then when we get home at maybe midnight, there can be another phone message asking us to be somewhere urgently, or even someone

[84] Smith and Sykes (n 79), 29.

> sitting in the front room waiting all evening for the chance to talk. How can we say what we do?[85]

One of tactics used by Black women of this era was to create alliances with groups that embraced an anti-racism platform, such as the Communist Party of Australia ('CPA'). At the beginning of her activism, Oodgeroo Noonuccal was drawn to the CPA because it was the only political party at the time that did not endorse the White Australia policy.[86] In the 1950s, Gladys O'Shane would also use her alliances with the CPA and the union movement to publicise the plight of Indigenous peoples who were institutionalised in Queensland's oppressive Reserves.[87]

In New South Wales, the formidable Pearl Gibbs began her long commitment to the struggle for Indigenous rights when she spoke out against the injustices suffered by women in domestic service.[88] Gibbs later became renowned for her involvement in the Aborigines Progressive Association,[89] which would hold the historic Day of Mourning protest in 1938.[90] Throughout her decades of activism, Gibbs cultivated a diverse group of allies. According to Stephanie Gilbert her network encompassed, 'prime ministers, attorneys-general, numerous members of parliament in New South Wales, waterfront and other unions, feminist groups, women's groups, and members of the media'.[91]

In the 1970s Indigenous women were among those who founded medical, legal and health services. The first Aboriginal-controlled medical service was established in the Sydney suburb of Redfern in 1971 by a small

[85] Ibid., 54–55.

[86] John Collins, 'Obituary: Oodgeroo of the Tribe Noonuccal' (1994) 18(1/2) *Aboriginal History*, 1.

[87] Sue Taffe, 'The Cairns Aborigines and Torres Strait Islander Advancement League and the Community of the Left' (2009) 97 *Labour History*, 149, 156.

[88] Rachel Standfield, Ray Peckham and John Nolan, 'Aunty Pearl Gibbs: Leading for Aboriginal Rights' in Joy Damousi, Kim Rubenstein and Mary Tomsic (eds), *Diversity in Leadership: Australian Women, Past and Present* (ANU Press, 2014), 53, 54.

[89] Stephanie Gilbert, '"Never Forgotten": Pearl Gibbs (Gambanyi)' in Anna Cole, Victoria Haskins and Fiona Paisley (eds), *Uncommon Ground: White Women in Aboriginal History* (Aboriginal Studies Press, 2005), 107, 109.

[90] Ibid., 110. The Day of Mourning was held in Sydney on Australia Day in 1938 to highlight the plight of Indigenous people during lavish celebrations for Australia's sesquicentenary.

[91] Ibid., 107.

group of community representatives, doctors and lawyers, in response to a health crisis brought about by endemic racism in the mainstream healthcare system.[92] According to Professor Gary Foley, some Indigenous patients would have preferred to die rather than face 'degrading humiliating treatment at the hands of non-Aboriginal health workers'.[93] At its inception in July 1971, the Redfern Aboriginal Medical Service ('AMS') was run by volunteers.[94] After much lobbying the AMS secured federal funding, which enabled it to employ a doctor, a nurse and a field officer, Shirley Smith.[95] In 1972, Naomi Mayers would be employed as the administrator.[96] Hailing from a family with a long commitment to the Indigenous struggle, Mayers would become recognised as a leader in Indigenous health.[97]

Indigenous women also established child-care services. In her history of Aboriginal activism in Redfern,[98] Johanna Perheentupa chronicled the story of the Murawina preschool and child-care centre. Established in 1973, Murawina grew from a breakfast program created by community leaders, the AMS and the Wayside Chapel out of recognition that many Indigenous children were going to school hungry.[99] Under the leadership of Black women, Murawina became a space where children were encouraged to take pride in their identity and culture. Murawina's program was holistic; accommodating the children's educational and emotional needs, providing assistance with housing, and making referrals to appropriate services.[100]

[92] Donnaleen Campbell and Rose Ellis, 'Models of Excellence in Indigenous Community Health: The Aboriginal Medical Service, Redfern' (1995) 19(4) *Aboriginal and Islander Health Worker Journal*, 4, 6.

[93] Gary Foley, 'Redfern Aboriginal Medical Service: 20 Years On' (1991) *Aboriginal and Islander Health Worker Journal*, 4.

[94] Ibid., 5.

[95] Campbell and Ellis (n 92), 6.

[96] Ibid.

[97] Leonarda Kovacic and Barbara Lemon, 'Mayers, Naomi Ruth (1941–)' *The Australian Women's Register* (20 May 2005), http://www.womenaustralia.info/biogs/AWE1172b.htm.

[98] Johanna Perheentupa, *Redfern: Aboriginal Activism in the 1970s* (Aboriginal Studies Press, 2020).

[99] Ibid., 132–134.

[100] Ibid., 140.

In summary, Indigenous women's outlaw culture is discernable in a diversity of relationships with the law. Women such as Walyer and Mary Ann Bugg seized their autonomy by operating outside of the law. Later outlaw women broke free from the shackles of protectionist legislation by running away and using their wits to evade detection by the authorities. Others worked within the law, and drew upon their experiential knowledge to provide for the most disadvantaged members of their communities.

As demonstrated in this part, expressions of Indigenous women's outlaw culture abound in historical accounts, life stories and oral histories. The following part will discuss another potential source of outlaw narratives, which is legal storytelling. The appearance of Indigenous women in legal storytelling represents a juncture between the themes of this chapter. On one hand, Indigenous women's voices are usually absent from judgments, suggesting that they have no agency in the story. On the other hand, however, there is a growing tradition within Indigenous women's outlaw culture of pursuing litigation with the aim of protecting one's community and Country.

Part Three: Indigenous Women and Legal Storytelling

Introduction

When Indigenous women emerge in judgments as parties and witnesses their voices are often missing. Sanitised of their connections to Country, family ties and legacies of the ruptures brought about by colonisation, they become mere silhouettes. Alternatively, Indigenous women are hidden behind representations that are so familiar to most Australians that they alone define reality. This denial of voice is at odds with the contributions that Indigenous women have made to democratising Australian law. In the closing decades of the twentieth century, a small number of Black women were able to marshal sufficient resources to initiate litigation that would hold powerful individuals, governments and corporations to account.

This part will begin by discussing two cases, at different times during Australia's history, in which the stories of Indigenous women were absent from the judgments. It will then provide examples of cases brought by courageous Black women who were able to harness the law to create spaces of safety. Finally, I will argue in favour of reimagining the stories of Indigenous women who appear in judgments, with the aim of casting light on instances of outlaw culture.

Absence of Voice

Tuckiar v R[101]

One of the cases that I studied at law school, which I have often reflected upon over the years was *Tuckiar v R*. The legal principles that we extracted from the case, which concerned the ethical obligations owed by advocates to their clients, were less important to me than the stories of those who appeared in the pages of the judgments. Tuckiar, whose real name was Dhakiyara Wirrpanda,[102] was an esteemed leader of the Yolngu of Arnhem Land in the Northern Territory. He was convicted of the murder of a police officer, Constable Albert McColl. In August 1933, McColl had been a member of a police party that travelled to the remote Woodah Island to investigate the deaths of some Japanese fishermen. Their arrival would change Dhakiyara's life irrevocably.

Soon after landing the party apprehended some Yolngu women.[103] Although the women were not suspected of committing any crime they were restrained in handcuffs.[104] After receiving word that a group of Yolngu had alighted nearby, the party dispersed. Some went to intercept the new arrivals. McColl, however, stayed with the women and the police trackers. McColl was not seen alive again. His body was found the following morning. McColl appeared to have died from a spear wound to his chest.[105]

The Crown's evidence against Dhakiyara consisted of confessions that he allegedly made to two Aboriginal men, Parriner and Harry. According to Parriner, Dhakiyara claimed to have seen McColl with one of his wives and the two communicated by sign language. Dhakiyara signalled

[101] *Tuckiar v R* (1934) 52 CLR 335.

[102] Ted Egan, *Justice All Their Own: The Caledon Bay and Woodah Island Killings 1932–1933* (Melbourne University Press, 1996).

[103] *Tuckiar v R* (1934) 52 CLR 335, 339.

[104] Ibid.

[105] Ibid.

to his wife to move and then he launched his spear at McColl.[106] McColl clutched the spear and fired his pistol three times. The confession made to Parriner was at variance with that allegedly made to Harry. Significantly, the latter claimed to have been told by Dhakiyara that he hid in the bush while McColl and his wife had sexual intercourse. Afterwards, McColl saw Dhakiyara and fired at him three times. After McColl reloaded his pistol, Dhakiyara threw his spear and hit him.[107]

Following a trial which was conducted in a language that he did not understand, Dhakiyara was found guilty of murder and sentenced to death. However, there were a number of anomalies that caused the trial to miscarry. Evidence of McColl's good character, which was inadmissible, was allowed in to protect McColl's reputation from the slur of having sexual relations with a Black woman.[108] The trial judge also gave directions to the jury that were calculated to cause prejudice to the accused.[109] Finally, after the jury delivered its verdict, Dhakiyara's counsel breached his obligations to his client by disclosing that Dhakiyara had privately revealed that the confession made to Parriner was correct.[110] Unsurprisingly, the High Court quashed the conviction. Sadly, Dhakiyara disappeared soon after his release from prison.

I have always been struck by the silence of the Indigenous women in the judgments. The Yolngu women were reduced to nameless 'lubras'.[111] Not one of them was called to give evidence of what they might have seen on the day that McColl lost his life. The actions of the police in placing the women in handcuffs were illegal, but barely raised a murmur.[112] Finally, the possibility that one of the women had sexual intercourse with McColl while she was deprived of her liberty did not appear to raise any concerns about impropriety on his part. We will never know what the women thought about the events on Woodah Island, or how their lives

[106] Ibid., 340.

[107] Ibid., 341.

[108] Ibid.

[109] Ibid., 344–346.

[110] Ibid., 346–347.

[111] Ibid., 339.

[112] Justice Starke considered that it was 'necessary for the police to capture and handcuff the lubras if they were to achieve the object of their expedition, but the rules of English law cannot be cited in support of their action'. *Tuckiar v R* (1934) 52 CLR 335, 352.

were impacted afterwards. But like their countrymen, they too would pass away without knowing what became of Dhakiyara.

Hales v Jamilmira[113]

For many Indigenous people, the Howard Government (1996–2007) will always be remembered for its resolve to wind back the clock and return to the former assimilation era. Howard and his ministers abandoned the policy of self-determination, which had been adopted by governments of all hues for decades. In its place was 'practical reconciliation', that is, a body of policies and programs which were aimed at achieving 'practical outcomes' in areas such as health, education and housing. The measures were isolated from the pursuit of greater rights for Indigenous people.[114] The impacts of practical reconciliation were devastating.

In its first year, the Howard Government culled the Indigenous affairs budget by over 400 million dollars.[115] Later, the *Native Title Act 1993* (Cth) was watered down.[116] Within a few years the national representative body, the Aboriginal and Torres Strait Islander Commission would also be gone[117]; denying Indigenous people an autonomous voice in Canberra. The battle lines were drawn not only over policy, but also the nation's identity. Attempts by the former Keating Government to engage with Indigenous perspectives of Australian history were roundly rejected by Howard.[118] In an act of mean spiritedness, he also refused to apologise to members of the Stolen Generations for the harms caused by being removed from their families.[119]

[113] *Hales v Jamilmira* [2003] 13 NTLR 14.

[114] Greg Crough, 'A Practical Critique of Practical Reconciliation: What Is the Reality of Indigenous Funding?' (2002) 45(1) *Australian Universities Review*, 4.

[115] John Gardiner-Garden, 'Overview of Indigenous Affairs: Part 2: 1992–2010' (Research Report, Commonwealth Parliamentary Library, 10 May 2011) https://www.aph.gov.au/about_parliament/parliamentary_departments/parliamentary_library/pubs/bn/1011/indigenousaffairs2.

[116] Ibid.

[117] Ibid.

[118] Nakari Thorpe, '7 Legacies of John Howard's Government' *NITV News* (online, 3 March 2016), https://www.sbs.com.au/nitv/the-point-with-stan-grant/article/2016/03/03/7-legacies-john-howards-government.

[119] 'The PM and Aboriginal Australia—A Timeline' *Crikey* (Melbourne, 12 October 2007), https://www.crikey.com.au/2007/10/12/the-pm-and-aboriginal-australia-a-timeline/.

As Indigenous people around the country watched hard fought for gains dissolve in Australia's capital, the community of Maningrida in the Northern Territory was about to feel the glare of the media's spotlight as a result of *Hales v Jamilmira*.[120] Jamilmira was a 49-year-old man who lived on an outstation in Maningrida. Several years previously he had entered into arrangements to marry the victim, who was fifteen years of age at the relevant time.

On 20 August 2001, Jamilmira approached the victim and told her to go to his home. After she declined he insisted, and she followed him into his home. Once inside his bedroom, the victim listened to a stereo and told Jamilmira to leave the bedroom door open. Jamilmira shut the door and soon after, he had sexual intercourse with the victim. The following day, the victim attempted to leave the outstation with some friends. Jamilmira responded by firing a shotgun into the air, scaring the victim and those who had attempted to help her escape.

Jamilmira was subsequently charged with one count of unlawful sexual intercourse with a female under the age of 16 years, and one count of discharging a firearm in a manner that was likely to endanger, annoy or frighten any person. In his record of interview with the police, Jamilmira conceded that he was aware that it was illegal for him to have intercourse with a fifteen-year-old girl. But he also claimed that under his law and custom, he had 'rights' to the victim's body because she was his 'promised wife'.[121] Jamilmira also justified his actions by reference to pressure that he allegedly received from the victim's relatives, who were concerned that she had begun 'prowling' in the evenings.[122]

Jamilmira pleaded guilty to both offences. In relation to the first count he was sentenced to 13 months imprisonment, to be suspended after four months.[123] In relation to the latter, he was sentenced to two months imprisonment.[124] On appeal to the Supreme Court of the Northern Territory, Jamilmira's sentence was substantially reduced. For the offence of having sex with an under-age girl, he was sentenced to a mere 24 hours

[120] *Hales v Jamilmira* [2003] 13 NTLR 14.

[121] Ibid., [6].

[122] Ibid., [16].

[123] Ibid., [1].

[124] Ibid.

imprisonment.[125] In relation to the firearm offence, he received 14 days imprisonment.[126] On a further appeal to the Northern Territory Court of Appeal, Jamilmira was sentenced to 12 months imprisonment for the former offence.[127] His sentence for the latter remained in place.

The decision spurred sensational media commentary.[128] My focus here, however, is not the voyeuristic coverage, but rather, the absence of Indigenous women's voices, beginning with that of the victim. Because Jamilmira pleaded guilty, she was spared the trauma of having to give evidence and undergo cross-examination. However, the victim's story was also missing. Only a small part of her victim impact statement appeared in the judgment of Martin CJ:

> I am angry for what he done. I was sad and upset. I think about it all the time. I always get angry with everyone. This makes me upset.[129]

When the extract from her statement is considered together with accepted facts, namely, the victim's initial reluctance to go to Jamilmira's house and her later attempt to escape, doubt is cast on the veracity of Jamilmira's assertions that he had acted appropriately and that there was an absence of coercion.[130] Jamilmira's representation of the victim as an unruly woman who had taken to 'prowling' like an alley cat, also escaped any real challenge.

Indigenous women's perspectives of Indigenous law were also absent from the judgments. The material before the Court in relation to Indigenous law consisted of evidence from an Indigenous man who was raised in Maningrida,[131] a pre-sentence report prepared by a male officer of

[125] Ibid., [2].

[126] Ibid.

[127] Ibid., [37].

[128] For example, see Andrew Bolt, 'Dark Side of Justice', *News.com.au* (17 September 2009), https://www.news.com.au/news/dark-side-of-justice/news-story/d6b12879afb5b8926b7045b700e744be?sv=67e672d47bfcc229e0d3ed54ca1b0acc.

[129] *Hales v Jamilmira* [2003] 13 NTLR 14, [26].

[130] Heather Douglas, '"She Knew What Was Expected of Her": The White Legal System's Encounter with Traditional Marriage' (2005) 13 *Feminist Legal Studies*, 181, 192.

[131] *Hales v Jamilmira* [2003] 13 NTLR 14, [12].

the Northern Territory's correctional services agency,[132] and a report put together by a white, female anthropologist.[133] Collectively, that material supported the assertion that Jamilmira's actions were sanctioned by Indigenous law. But as Cripps and Taylor later observed, the silencing of Indigenous women 'should not be interpreted as a sign that [they] were in agreement with what was articulated'[134] by those whose voices were heard. We will never know what the women in Jamilmira's community actually thought of his actions or if their interpretations of Indigenous law were at variance with his, because no one involved in the case saw fit to ask them.

Harnessing the Law

The erasure of Black female voices from the above cases is in contrast to a growing tradition of Indigenous women using the law to protect themselves, their loved ones and Country. This part will discuss three examples where outlaw women sparked 'David and Goliath' battles in Australia's superior courts, and in the process, challenged the judiciary to live up to the ideal of equality before the law. It is impossible to acknowledge all of the Black women who have contributed to this dimension of outlaw culture. However, I hope that the brief discussion below will inspire other scholars to cast a lens over the contributions made by Black women to the development of Australian law.

Onus v Alcoa[135]

Ten years before the High Court delivered its epoch-making decision in *Mabo v Queensland (No 2)*,[136] two Black women achieved a remarkable legal victory of their own. In 1981, Sandra Onus and Christina Frankland commenced an action against the mining company, Alcoa in the Victorian Supreme Court. The women, who were members of the Gunditjmara People, sought to block the construction of an aluminium smelter in their

[132] Ibid., [13].

[133] Ibid., [19].

[134] Kyllie Cripps and Caroline Taylor, 'White Man's Law, Traditional Law, Bullshit Law: Customary Marriage Revisited' (2009) 10 *Balayi: Culture, Law and Colonialism*, 59, 68.

[135] *Onus v Alcoa* (1981) 149 CLR 27.

[136] *Mabo v Queensland (No 2)* (1992) 175 CLR 1.

Country in Portland, Victoria. They argued that the smelter would interfere with their custodianship of ancient relics, in breach of s 21 of the *Archaeological and Aboriginal Relics Preservation Act 1972* (Vic).[137]

In order to have standing to bring an action for the violation of a public right, plaintiffs must show that they have a special interest in the subject-matter.[138] The Victorian Supreme Court held that the women had not made a prima facie case for standing to sue to prevent a breach of the Act. The women's appeal to the Full Court of the Supreme Court was unsuccessful. However, they would eventually achieve victory in the High Court. The majority recognised that the women had standing to commence an action to restrain a breach of the Act, to protect relics that were of cultural and spiritual significance to their people.[139]

The women's success prompted the Victorian Premier, John Cain to make a significant offer. In exchange for withdrawing their action against Alcoa, they were promised a package of measures that included ownership of the former Lake Condah Mission, which had previously been home to generations of the Gunditjmara.[140] In 1951 the reserve was revoked and the lands were relinquished to a soldiers settlement scheme.[141] Tragically, applications for land that were brought by members of the Gunditjmara who had served in the Australian Army were rejected.[142] The package that was negotiated as a result of the women's legal action delivered belated redress for such injustices.

The action also provided valuable experience that prepared the Gunditjmara for the complex and often unwieldy recognition process contained in the *Native Title Act 1993* (Cth). Their efforts culminated in a consent determination in 2007, which recognised the Gunditjmara's native title over 1400 square kilometres of land that included national

[137] Tannetje L. Bryant, 'Recent Developments on Locus Standi: Onus v Alcoa of Australia Ltd' (1982) 8 *Monash University Law Review*, 186, 190.

[138] Ibid., 186.

[139] *Onus v Alcoa* (1981) 149 CLR 27.

[140] Jessica K. Weir, *The Gunditjmara Land Justice Story* (Australian Institute of Aboriginal and Torres Strait Islander Studies, 2009), 14.

[141] Ibid., 10.

[142] Ibid., 11.

parks, vacant crown land, rivers and creeks.[143] Today, the action initiated by Sandra Onus and Christina Frankland is celebrated as a milestone by the Gunditjmara in their struggle for land justice. But in historical accounts of the land rights movement, their impressive victory is often overlooked.[144]

Roach v Electoral Commissioner[145]

Vickie Roach is the epitome of the outlaw woman who uses the law to protect the rights of marginalised people, and as a result, democratises the law. She challenged the validity of amendments that were made to the *Commonwealth Electoral Act 1918* in 2006, which disqualified all persons serving sentences of imprisonment from voting in federal elections.[146] Two years earlier, the disqualification had been applied only to those who were serving sentences of three years or longer.[147] Vickie Roach challenged the validity of both the 2006 and 2004 provisions in the High Court.

Vickie Roach advanced a number of grounds in support of her claim; including the assertion that the provisions were contrary to ss. 7 and 24 of the *Constitution*, which require the Senate and members of the House of Representatives to 'be directly chosen by the people'.[148] She also argued that the legislation was inconsistent with either the implied freedom of political communication or the implied freedom of political participation.[149] The majority of the High Court found that the 2006 amendments were invalid, while upholding the validity of the 2004 provisions.[150]

Vickie Roach's success is all the more impressive when one considers that she was in custody at the time of her action. In an interview soon after the High Court handed down its decision, her solicitor, Philip Lynch

[143] Ibid., 21.

[144] Ibid., 15.

[145] *Roach v Electoral Commissioner* (2007) 233 CLR 162.

[146] Ibid.

[147] Ibid.

[148] *Roach v Electoral Commissioner*, (2007) 11(3) *Australian Indigenous Law Review*, 70.

[149] Ibid.

[150] Ibid., 71.

revealed that it was Vicki Roach who provided the necessary impetus to begin the action, despite her incarceration:

> She chose us rather than us choosing her. Vickie came to us through the prisoner advocacy networks as a woman with an interest in and commitment to human rights and freedoms and, in particular, her rights as a prisoner.[151]

In a later interview with the ABC, Vickie Roach shared her life story.[152] As an infant she became a member of the Stolen Generations. By the time that she was 11-years-old Vickie had been taken into a children's home,[153] and during her teenage years, she lived on the streets of Sydney. By the time that she was 17-years-old Vickie was in jail.[154] On the night of her eighteenth birthday, she witnessed a friend die after receiving appalling treatment from prison officers.[155] Many would have been broken by such adversity, but not Vickie Roach.

Today, she is an advocate for the abolition of prisons. In her interview with the ABC, Vickie Roach pointed out that rather than invest in a cruel system that dehumanises and causes further trauma for people who have already experienced marginalisation, governments should fund 'healing places':

> A better system to me would be healing places, particularly for Aboriginal women … But for all people, we have to heal rather than punish. People meting out vengeance and punishment and cruelty will only reap bad things in the future for society.[156]

[151] Karen Kissane, 'Former Delinquent Takes on Government and Wins' *The Age* (online, 31 August 2007), https://www.theage.com.au/national/former-delinquent-takes-on-government-and-wins-20070831-ge5pqu.html.

[152] Michael Dulaney, 'Vickie Roach Saw Her First Death in Custody at 18. She's Spent the Decades Since Fighting to Abolish Prisons' *ABC News* (9 July 2020), https://www.abc.net.au/news/2020-07-09/vickie-roach-on-indigenous-deaths-in-custody-prison-abolition/12430850.

[153] Ibid.

[154] Ibid.

[155] Ibid.

[156] Dulaney (n 152).

Eatock v Bolt[157]

For those outside of Australia, Andrew Bolt may not be a familiar name. For most Australians, however, he is one of the most powerful conservative commentators in the country. As a columnist with the *Herald Sun* and host of the *The Bolt Report* on Sky News, he has cultivated a significant following. In 2009 he used his platform to condemn prominent Indigenous people who had a fair complexion for identifying as Indigenous. Bolt also implied that the individuals were politically motivated to identify as Indigenous or did so to enhance their career prospects.[158]

The tone of the articles was incendiary and sarcastic. By way of example, in one article, 'It's so hip to be black' he lashed out at a 'whole new fashion' in which people whose connection with their Indigenous heritage was tenuous had freely chosen to identify.[159] As a person who also has fair skin, I can imagine how devastated I would be if a stranger publicly attacked my claim to the identity that was given to me by those who reared me. However, I doubt that I would have the courage to challenge my aggressor in an open court. Nine individuals did have the bravery to do exactly that.[160]

In an action led by the late Pat Eatock they argued that Bolt and his publisher, the Herald and Weekly Times had infringed s 18C of the *Racial Discrimination Act 1975* (Cth) ('RDA'), which provides:

> It is unlawful for a person to do an act, otherwise than in private, if:
>
> (a) The act is reasonably likely, in all the circumstances, to offend, insult, humiliate or intimidate another person or a group of people; and
> (b) The act is done because of the race, colour or national or ethnic origin of the other person or of some or all of the people in the group.

The complainants were vindicated when Bromberg J. found that Bolt and his publisher had contravened s. 18C. Both were restrained from

[157] *Eatock v Bolt* (2011) 197 FCR 261.

[158] Ibid., [37].

[159] Ibid., [24].

[160] They were Pat Eatock, Anita Heiss, Mark McMillan, Wayne Atkinson, Graham Atkinson, Bindi Cole, Geoff Clark, Larissa Behrendt and Leeanne Enoch.

republishing the offensive articles and the Herald and Weekly Times were ordered to publish a corrective notice.[161]

In what was no doubt a harrowing experience, the complainants gave evidence that they had been raised by their families as Indigenous and rejected the claim that they had used their identity inappropriately. One of the themes that emerged in their evidence was a desire to protect other Indigenous people, who also had a fair complexion, from being fearful of claiming their heritage. For example, Professor Larissa Behrendt, a Distinguished Professor and filmmaker, was humiliated by Bolt who implied that she was 'not Aboriginal enough'.[162] In her evidence, Professor Behrendt revealed a desire to protect younger, vulnerable Indigenous people from similar attacks.[163]

The award-winning novelist, Anita Heiss, was also a complainant. In her memoir,[164] she reflected on her motivation for pursuing relief under the RDA, as opposed to suing Bolt and his publisher in defamation. Heiss explained that the latter was not the most appropriate form of action because it was concerned only with damage to an individual's reputation. In her view, the harm caused by the articles extended to her entire community, and for that reason, the RDA was the most appropriate forum:

> I was conscious that while we were a group of nine plaintiffs, we were also representing all those Aboriginal people likely to have been offended by the article. I was never interested in monetary compensation, which a defamation case would have sought to achieve. I wanted the publication of under-researched, race-based information to end. The RDA was the only way to ensure that this might happen.[165]

The cases discussed in this part teach us much about the treatment of Indigenous women in legal storytelling. Most obviously, they reveal the absence of Indigenous women's stories. The Yolngu women who featured

[161] Adrienne Stone, 'The Ironic Aftermath of *Eatock v Bolt*' (2014–2015) 38(3) *Melbourne University Law Review*, 926, 938.

[162] *Eatock v Bolt* (2011) 197 FCR 261, [125].

[163] Ibid., [128].

[164] Anita Heiss, *Am I Black Enough for You?* (Bantam, 2012).

[165] Ibid., 128.

in *Tuckiar*[166] must have been terrified when the police party restrained them in handcuffs. But their fear was of little consequence to the powerful white men of the High Court. The voices of the young victim and senior women in her community were also missing from *Hales v Jamilmira.*[167] As a result, Jamilmira's story and his interpretation of Indigenous law were privileged.

The latter cases reveal the foresight and ingenuity of outlaw women. Sandra Onus and Christina Frankland persuaded the majority of the High Court that they had standing to sue to enforce cultural heritage legislation.[168] Their action led to the creation of a beneficial settlement and prepared the Gunditjmara for the rigours of the native title recognition process. Vickie Roach not only sought to defend her own right to vote, but she also fought to safeguard the rights of all prisoners to participate in Australian democracy. Finally, women such as Larissa Behrendt and Anita Heiss sought to use the RDA as a shield to protect other Indigenous people from being afraid of asserting their identity.

The latter cases also suggest that judgments are a potential wellspring of outlaw stories. However, because the voices of Indigenous women rarely feature in legal storytelling, other sources of information are required to piece together their narratives. In the following chapter, I will show how the stories of Indigenous women who emerge in judgments can be constructed as speculative biography. Speculative biography is a means of writing life stories by not only working from evidence on the public record, but also, making 'educated guesses'[169] to complete gaps in knowledge about the subject's life. I will demonstrate that speculative biography is an ideal vehicle for casting light on the narratives of Indigenous women outlaws. Archival records will tell only part of their stories, and even then, surviving documents will be imbued with the biases of those who produced them.[170] Furthermore, the 'emotional responses,

[166] (1934) 52 CLR 335.

[167] [2003] 13 NTLR 14.

[168] *Onus v Alcoa* (1981) 149 CLR 27.

[169] Donna Lee Brien, 'Australian Speculative Biography: Recovering Forgotten Lives' in Dallas John Baker, Donna Lee Brien and Nike Sulway (eds), *Recovering History Through Fact and Fiction: Forgotten Lives* (Cambridge Scholars Publishing, 2017), 11, 15.

[170] Katerina Bryant, 'Speculative Biography and Countering Archival Absences of Women Clowns in the Circus' (2021) 18(1) *Life Writing*, 31, 32.

thoughts and motivations'[171] of the women are likely to be absent from such records. Speculative biography enables the writer to imagine those elements to construct a complete life story.[172]

The following chapter will piece together the story of an Indigenous woman, Eliza Woree, whose name appeared in the judgments of the Supreme Court of Queensland in the case of *Dempsey v Rigg*.[173] By drawing upon archival materials, newspaper articles and historical accounts, I will imagine her life before the decision, and speculate how the case may have impacted upon her life thereafter. This process will reveal that Eliza was a pioneer of outlaw culture who attempted to create a life of her own, despite the various obstacles confronted by Black women of her generation.

Conclusion

Degrading caricatures of Indigenous women belonged to a system of ideas that buttressed the foundation myth, that is, the narrative that Australia was created through the heroic endeavours of white men. Representations of the jezebel, the savage and the wretched victim of Black male violence, all served to obscure the realities of a brutal invasion. They also became the means through which generations of white Australians came to know Indigenous women.

However, Indigenous women have never been the submissive prey of colonisation. Despite the horrors of invasion, and later, the erosion of personal freedoms under the policies of protection and assimilation, Indigenous women created ingenious means to reclaim their autonomy. Some outlaw women empowered themselves by entering relationships with male bushrangers. Others risked their liberty to take strike action. Three young girls would break free of the iron grip of the authorities and walk 1600 kilometres to return to the arms of their loved ones. Other outlaw women drew upon whatever resources they could find to care for the most vulnerable people within their families and communities. With the emergence of the policy of self-determination in the 1970s, outlaw

[171] Brien (n 169), 16.

[172] Ibid.

[173] *Dempsey v Rigg* [1914] St R Qd 245.

women were among those who established community-controlled organisations that provided services for people who had suffered long histories of neglect.

This chapter has revealed how outlaw culture is embedded in historical accounts, life stories and evidence received by inquiries. Another potential source of outlaw narratives is legal storytelling. Indigenous women who emerge in judgments as parties and witnesses are invariably muted and relegated to the background. This is at odds with an emerging tradition within outlaw culture of using the law as a tool of empowerment. In the following chapter, I will show how the stories of Indigenous women who appear in legal storytelling can be imagined so as to cast light on their agency and resilience.

CHAPTER 4

Eliza Woree: An Early Pioneer of Outlaw Culture

Abstract This chapter will imagine the story of Eliza Woree, an Aboriginal woman who featured in the backdrop to the decision of the Supreme Court of Queensland in *Dempsey v Rigg* [1914] St R Qd 245. Isaac Rigg committed the offence of unlawfully employing an Aboriginal, in breach of the provisions of the *Aboriginals Protection and Restriction of the Sale of Opium Act 1897* (Qld), when he employed Eliza in the absence of official sanction. Through the device of speculative biography, Eliza's life story will be pieced together. When her voice is brought from the margins to the centre, Eliza emerges as a pioneer of outlaw culture.

Keywords Indigenous women · Legal storytelling · Reimagined voices

Introduction

Early outlaw women were largely invisible to those who were responsible for upholding the law. Treated as problems to be controlled, their opinions and aspirations counted for little. In spite of the various degradations suffered by Aboriginal women as a result of colonisation, some were able to create new lives and exercise a degree of autonomy. This chapter will imagine the story of one such outlaw woman, Eliza Woree, who played

N. Watson, *Aboriginal Women, Law and Critical Race Theory*, Palgrave Studies in Race, Ethnicity, Indigeneity and Criminal Justice, https://doi.org/10.1007/978-3-030-87327-1_4

a critical role in the backdrop to the decision of the Supreme Court of Queensland in *Dempsey v Rigg*.[1]

In December 1913, Isaac Rigg of White Rock in Cairns employed Eliza to perform washing and ironing. A short time later, Rigg was charged with unlawfully employing an Aboriginal under s. 14 of the *Aboriginals Protection and Restriction of the Sale of Opium Act 1897* (Qld). Section fourteen provided:

> Any person who, except under the provisions of any Act or Regulations thereunder in force in Queensland, employs an aboriginal or a female half-caste, otherwise than in accordance with the provisions of this Act or the Regulations, or suffers or permits an aboriginal or a female half-caste to be in or upon any house or premises in his occupation or under his control, shall be guilty of an offence against this Act, and shall be liable, on conviction, to a penalty not exceeding fifty pounds and not less than ten pounds, or to imprisonment for any term not exceeding six months.

Two months earlier Eliza had married Joe Andrews, who was a 'Malay' and a 'native of Batavia', now called Jakarta.[2] Rigg argued that as a consequence of the marriage, Eliza ceased to be an Aboriginal within the meaning of the *Aboriginals Protection and Restriction of the Sale of Opium Acts 1897 to 1901* (Qld). The Supreme Court of Queensland disagreed. Chief Justice Cooper recognised that the Court's decision might have adverse consequences for the husbands of Aboriginal women,[3] who could attract liability under s. 14 by merely living with their spouse. However, the Court was bound to give the words of the legislation their 'natural and ordinary meaning'.[4]

Although she was at the centre of the case, Eliza Woree's story was entirely absent from the judgments. By drawing upon historical research, newspaper reports, oral histories and archival materials, this chapter will piece together her narrative. It is a tale of loss and degrading subjugation. But it also casts light on the tenacity of the Aboriginal women who personify outlaw culture. After surviving the brutalities of invasion and

[1] *Dempsey v Rigg* [1914] St R Qd 245.

[2] Ibid.

[3] Ibid., 248.

[4] Ibid.

dispossession, women such as Eliza Woree went on to build new lives, and seized agency however they could.

This chapter will be divided into three parts. In part one I will imagine Eliza's childhood, which coincided with the invasion of the Bama, the rainforest people of tropical north Queensland. This was a time of great violence, when Aboriginal people were hunted down by the Native Police who murdered with impunity. Part two will consider how the Act and the common law combined to deprive Eliza of autonomy in relation to her employment and marriage. Finally, part three will begin six years after the Supreme Court's decision, when Eliza was living in 'Malaytown', an informal settlement on the outskirts of Cairns. For a brief period of time, Eliza achieved the impressive feat of creating an independent life for herself.

Part One: Eliza's Childhood

Introduction

Sadly, I was unable to find any record of Eliza's own testimony. To the best of my knowledge, there is no surviving photograph of her either. All that remains of Eliza Woree's existence are bare assertions scattered in a handful of documents that now reside in the Queensland Archives. Marrying those fragments of her life with historical accounts of the north Queensland frontier helps us to imagine Eliza's formative years.

The official record begins with Eliza's marriage to Joe Andrews. The two exchanged their vows on 18 September 1913 in the District Registrar's Office, Cairns.[5] The Marriage Certificate reveals that Eliza's place of birth was Woree, Cairns.[6] But it does not disclose anything of her family history or the language that she and her loved ones spoke. The Marriage Certificate reveals the name of Eliza's father—Billy Woree. But no information was entered concerning her mother. Likewise, we do not know if Eliza had any siblings. Finally, the Marriage Certificate provides that Eliza's age in 1913 was thirty; making her year of birth 1883. Although, this age is at variance with correspondence from the Cairns District Inspector of Police, which estimated Eliza's age as

[5] Queensland Marriage Certificate, Registration Number 1913/522 2055.

[6] Ibid.

'about twenty'.[7] Assuming the age recorded in the Marriage Certificate is correct, then Eliza came into the world only a few years after the commencement of the invasion of lands that had been held by generations of Aboriginal people who spoke the Djabugay and Yidiny languages.

Life on the Northern Frontier

In the first week of October 1876 the town of Cairns was established,[8] providing a convenient port for settlers who pursued their fortunes on north Queensland's gold fields. Over the ensuing years, Aboriginal people would be further dispossessed by pastoralists and farmers. Aboriginal people vehemently resisted the invaders over many years. They were able to take advantage of terrain which was unsuitable for travelling on horseback, and as a consequence, the Bama 'held out longer than was possible elsewhere'.[9]

The invaders retaliated through means that included poisoning,[10] and retribution at the hands of the Native Police. One notorious massacre within the Cairns district was perpetrated a year after Eliza was born. The killing spree was later relayed by one of the perpetrators, Jack Kane:

> … [i]n 1884 he took part in a police raid which lasted a week, culminating in a round up at Skull Pocket and others following at Mulgrave River and near the Four Mile [Woree]. At Skull Pocket police officers and native trackers surrounded a camp of Idinji [Yidinji] blacks before dawn, each man armed with a rifle and revolver. At dawn one man fired into their camp and the natives rushed away in three other directions. They were easy running shots, close up. The native police rushed in with their scrub knives and killed off the children. A few years later a man loaded up a whole case of skulls and took them away as specimens. [Old Jack stated] 'I didn't mind the killing of the "bucks" but I didn't quite like them braining the kids'.

[7] Letter from the Cairns District Inspector of Police to the Chief Protector of Aboriginals, 4 July 1913, Queensland State Archives, Eliza and Joe Andrews Marriages, 1913/1345, Item ID 336450.

[8] Timothy Bottoms, *Cairns City of the South Pacific: A History 1770–1995* (Bunu Bunu Press, 2015), 66.

[9] Matthew Daniel McCormack Richards, 'Race around Cairns: Representations, Perceptions and Realities of Race in the Trinity Bay District 1876–1908' (PhD thesis, James Cook University, 2010), 121.

[10] Ibid., 122.

> From the Skull Pocket the raiders journeyed to the Mulgrave & again at [the] Four Mile, and shot other natives, some of them with wounds received in the raid at Skull Pocket'.[11] (footnotes omitted)

It was also in 1884 that a massacre took place at Irvinebank, south-west of Cairns. The evidence provided to an inquiry into the killings was reported in detail in *The Queenslander.*[12] According to witnesses, a group of troopers led by one Sub-Inspector Nichols arrived at Irvinebank on 15 October.[13] Within days the partially burnt bodies of an elderly man, two women and a child were found. One witness described the victims as 'inoffensive creatures' who had been asleep when the Native Police surrounded them.[14] Sub-Inspector Nichols and the troopers were subsequently dismissed, but none were charged with murder.[15]

It is a certainty that Eliza and her loved ones would have been aware of the violence of the Native Police, which did not cease its operations until 1911.[16] However, it was not only the Native Police that posed a threat to Aboriginal children such as Eliza. They were also vulnerable to kidnapping. In the Cairns district, Aboriginal children were regularly stolen by settlers for use as household servants.[17] Those who were spared from abduction faced a perilous future alongside their adult relatives.

With their capacity to fight dwindling and their access to food and water precarious, Aboriginal people had little choice but to broker a co-existence with the settlers. Across Queensland Aboriginal people were gradually allowed to lead a wretched existence on the borders of Queensland's burgeoning townships. According to Reynolds, by the end of the nineteenth century ramshackle camps had been built on the fringes of virtually all of Queensland's towns.[18] The most dire problem confronting

[11] Timothy Bottoms, *Conspiracy of Silence: Queensland's Frontier Killing Times* (Allen & Unwin, 2013), 147–148.

[12] 'The Irvinebank Massacre', *The Queenslander* (20 December 1884), 992, http://nla.gov.au/nla.news-article23977061.

[13] Ibid.

[14] Ibid.

[15] Ibid.

[16] Bottoms (n 8), 77.

[17] Richards (n 9), 153.

[18] Henry Reynolds, 'Townspeople and Fringe-Dwellers' in Henry Reynolds (ed), *Race Relations in North Queensland* (History Department, James Cook University, 1978), 167.

those who lived in the camps was a lack of access to nutrition,[19] forcing many to beg, thieve and enter into prostitution.

Life on the margins of colonial society was characterised not only by scarcity, but also instability. The historian, J. W. Collinson described the tragic circumstances of one camp on the banks of Lily Creek in Cairns:

> Ten years had sufficed to bring about all the degradation civilisation could bestow; and in return for all they had lost, the Government doled out a blanket on the 24th May each year. For the rest they begged and did a little wood and water-carrying for a miserable existence. The camp was a nondescript collection of mia-mias, built of bags, old kerosene tins and bark, with a population of aboriginals and skinny and noisy curs. The men scavenged the town, but became a menace to lonely housewives, and it became necessary to shift them from town boundaries.[20]

Homeless and often teetering on the brink of starvation, many had little choice but to provide labour in exchange for rations. In time, northern townships became heavily dependent upon Aboriginal workers. In his history of the north Queensland frontier, Loos drew upon a first-hand account of the demand for Aboriginal labour in Cooktown:

> The wife of the Clerk of the Court is calling one black girl. 'Come on, Annie, quickly, it's Saturday, I have a lot of work for you today, you have to sweep through all the house for me'.
> 'Tobacco, missy, just a little bit!'
> 'Afterwards, Annie, as much as you like, afterwards; but now get on with it!'
> And elsewhere: Long Ah Kong, the jovial plump Chinese is beckoning to a black lad, while carefully tucking up his long plait: 'Billy, lad, come and sweep my store for me. I'll give you a lovely watermelon!'
> There is a third, Tommy, who does not need to be told what to do. He has some wood to split every morning for C., the publican, and he doesn't mind doing it, because the reward is well and truly worth it … beer!'[21]

[19] Ibid., 170.

[20] J. W. Collinson, *Early Days of Cairns* (Smith & Paterson, 1939), 65.

[21] Noel Loos, *Invasion and Resistance: Aboriginal-European Relations on the North Queensland Frontier 1861–1897* (Boolarong Press, 2nd ed, 2017), 163–165.

It is doubtful that Eliza ever had an opportunity to go to school. In 1896 the Queensland Education Department adopted a policy of denying entry to Aboriginal students, together with other 'coloured' children.[22] According to the Chief Clerk of the Department, schooling was of no use to Aboriginal children, who required 'teaching in religion, moral duty, decent behaviour, and habits of perseverance in settled industry'.[23] Rather than attend school, it is more likely that Eliza became a casual labourer.

Aboriginal child labourers of Eliza's era were arguably the state's most vulnerable workers. Often expected to perform physically demanding tasks, such children were rarely paid in wages and girls in particular, were exposed to sexual abuse. The powerlessness of such workers was brought into stark relief by the tragic story of 'Maggie'.[24] At the tender age of eleven Maggie arrived in the mining town of Thornborough, 80 kilometres west of Cairns, in search of work.[25] By the time that she was in her early teens, Maggie was working for the Nicholls family as a domestic servant. What little is known about Maggie revolves around her brutal killing at the hands of her employer, William Nicholls in 1887.[26]

Days before her death Maggie had left the Nicholls home and refused to return. In retaliation, William Nicholls struck several blows to Maggie's head with a stick 'as thick as a shovel handle'.[27] Maggie was not taken to a hospital to receive treatment for her injuries. Instead, she was laid down on the ground of the family's fowl house. William Nicholls subsequently beat Maggie; her cries being heard by several witnesses. Three days later, one Constable Montgomery found the unconscious Maggie in the fowl house. She was finally taken to a hospital, but it was too late to save her.[28]

Although Eliza escaped the tragic fate suffered by Maggie, the world of her childhood was brutal and volatile. It is a certainty that the adults around her carried enormous grief over the loss of Country, and deep

[22] Bottoms (n 8), 216.

[23] Loos (n 21), 168.

[24] Gary Highland, 'Aborigines, Europeans and the Criminal Law: Two Trials at the Northern Supreme Court, Townsville, April 1888' (1990) 14 (1/2) *Aboriginal History*, 182.

[25] Ibid., 186.

[26] Ibid.

[27] Ibid.

[28] Ibid.

psychological scars from the violence of the frontier. Cut off from the sources of sustenance that had been accessed by countless generations of their forebears, it is likely that Eliza and her loved ones experienced periods of hunger. Denied an education, it is probable that she worked as a casual labourer. But despite the various hardships suffered by children such as Eliza, they endured. Their determination to survive in a world that consistently denied their humanity is redolent of extraordinary resilience.

Part Two: Eliza's Adulthood

Introduction

By the time that Eliza reached maturity, Cairns bustled with infrastructure and industry. According to Timothy Bottoms, at the turn of the twentieth century, Cairns had a stock exchange, a tramway, 16 hotels, grocers and drapers.[29] However, living conditions were harsh. In his unpublished PhD thesis on the role of race in early Cairns, Richards depicted a town that was rife with poor sanitation and residents who were prone to ill health:

> Cairns was built upon and surrounded by swampy ground; it had no reticulated water supply, systems of drainage, sewerage or garbage removal; stagnant pools of horribly corrupted water lay everywhere for much of the year; waste piled up in back yards or was shoved beneath houses; closets overflowed their excremental contents; rats roamed in their thousands and for most of the year the humid air rang with mosquitos swimming in their pestilential millions. Its early decades had been marked by periodic outbreaks of deadly, inadequately understood and frequently misdiagnosed diseases arising within a largely transient population encumbered by bad diet and hard living conditions.[30] (footnotes omitted)

In the event of sickness, it is not a certainty that Eliza would have received medical care, as it was common for hospitals to refuse to admit Aboriginal patients.[31] Their exclusion from hospitals was but one of many indignities suffered by Aboriginal people as a result of their lowly place on the racial hierarchy. According to Russell McGregor, the hierarchy

[29] Bottoms (n 8), 288–290.

[30] Richards (n 9), 98.

[31] Loos (n 21), 80.

in northern townships such as Cairns posited Europeans at the apex, trailed by Japanese and Chinese residents on the second rung, followed by Malays and Javanese, Pacific Islanders and then, Torres Strait Islanders. Aboriginal people were relegated to the bottom step.[32] The racial hierarchy was manifest in various aspects of daily life, such as the allocation of labour, the payment of wages and property relations.[33]

Eliza's daily life was circumscribed not only by the informal rules of the racial hierarchy. She was also subject to the provisions of the *Aboriginals Protection and Restriction of the Sale of Opium Act 1897* (Qld). This legislation gave rise to a harsh and invasive regime that deprived generations of the freedom of movement and the ability to maintain family bonds. Aboriginal women suffered additional burdens as a result of the sexism that imbued both the Act and its administration.

Employment

By the time of her marriage to Joe Andrews, Eliza was employed as a housemaid by one Mrs Steele.[34] This is not surprising, given that domestic service was the most common form of employment for Aboriginal girls and women during the earlier part of the twentieth century.[35] We will never know whether Eliza freely entered into her employment with Mrs Steele. According to the historian, Jackie Huggins most Aboriginal people of this era had 'little choice' in choosing their employers.[36] Such decisions were typically made by the white men who performed the role of 'protector'.

[32] Russell McGregor, 'Drawing the Local Colour Line' (2012) 47(3) *The Journal of Pacific History*, 329, 332.

[33] Michael Woods, 'Rural Cosmopolitanism at the Frontier? Chinese Farmers and Community Relations in Northern Queensland, c. 1890–1920' (2018) 49(1) *Australian Geographer*, 107, 115.

[34] Letter from the Cairns District Inspector of Police to the Chief Protector of Aboriginals, 4 July 1913, Queensland State Archives, Eliza and Joe Andrews—Marriages, 1913/1345, Item ID 33650.

[35] Meg Parsons, 'Creating a Hygienic Dorm: The Refashioning of Aboriginal Women and Children and the Politics of Racial Classification in Queensland 1920s–40s' (2012) 14(2) *Health and History*, 112, 123.

[36] Jackie Huggins, 'White Aprons, Black Hands: Aboriginal Women Domestic Servants in Queensland' (1995) 69 *Labour History*, 188.

Eliza was probably subject to an employment agreement regulated by the provisions of the *Aboriginals Protection and Restriction of the Sale of Opium Act 1897* (Qld). Under s. 15 of the Act, any person who wished to employ an 'aboriginal or female half-caste' had to seek the acquiescence of a protector, and enter into an agreement with the intended employee in the presence of a justice of the peace or a member of the police force. The agreement was to cover matters such as the nature of the tasks to be performed, remuneration and accommodation.[37] Those who were employed pursuant to the Act were also subject to the ongoing supervision of a protector, who was empowered to carry out inspections and make any further inquiries that he considered necessary.[38]

The requirement to enter into formal agreements was bitterly resented by many employers. Such umbrage found resonance in the parliamentary debates concerning the passage of amendments[39] to the *Aboriginals Protection and Restriction of the Sale of Opium Act 1897* (Qld) in 1901. Although s. 15 was contained in the original Act, some members took advantage of the opportunity to air the grievances of employers. Perhaps the most odious complaint was made by the member for Burke, Mr Maxwell who lamented that there had been instances in his own district where:

> people who have reared blackboys from piccaninnies have had the boys taken from them and have not been granted permits. I know of one case in particular where a person had a boy for fifteen years, and he was refused a permit to employ an aboriginal.[40]

Maxwell's lack of compassion for children who had been deprived of parental affection and raised so that they knew only servitude, remains chilling over a century later.

Just as we do not know if Eliza voluntarily entered into the employment of Mrs Steele, it is impossible to determine if Eliza was treated with a modicum of fairness. In popular culture throughout the twentieth century, the white mistress was often represented as the 'good fella

[37] *Aboriginals Protection and Restriction of the Sale of Opium Act 1897* (Qld) s. 15.

[38] Ibid., s. 16.

[39] *Aboriginals Protection and Restriction of the Sale of Opium Bill 1901* (Qld).

[40] Queensland, *Parliamentary Debates*, Legislative Assembly, 30 July 1901, 211–212 (Mr Maxwell).

missus'[41]; a maternal figure who rescued the Aboriginal woman in her employ from the clutches of her violent Black husband.[42] The most renowned 'good fella missus' was Aeneas (Jeannie) Gunn, mistress of the Elsey Cattle Station in the Northern Territory, otherwise known as the 'never-never'.[43] In her writing, Gunn depicted her domestic servants as infantile beings who merrily performed their chores under her benevolent supervision.[44]

Such representations are at odds with first-hand accounts of former domestic servants. In common with many other Aboriginal families, my own has stories about the harsh treatment endured by loved ones at the hands of their former employers. One such story belonged to my great grandmother, Granny Roberts. My memories of our beautiful matriarch consist of images of a tiny, softly spoken woman who shared what little she possessed with others who were in need. As I grew into adulthood, older members of our family occasionally shared stories about Granny Roberts' childhood. I remember learning about how Granny Roberts was sent to work on a farm while she was still a child herself. Today, I struggle to imagine how hard it would have been for Granny Roberts to be removed from her loved ones, and compelled to work long hours for a mistress who was prone to violence. Somehow, Granny Roberts was unscathed by such cruelty, and grew into a much cherished member of the Aboriginal community in Brisbane.

Whether Eliza's mistress, Mrs Steele was a 'good fella missus' or not will never be known. But it is a certainty that the work undertaken by Eliza was demanding. According to Huggins, Aboriginal domestic servants typically worked 15-hour days, performing tasks that included washing, ironing, cleaning, butchering livestock and drawing water.[45] Huggins' portrayal of domestic service as both gruelling and exploitative, finds resonance in observations made by the former Chief Protector of Aboriginals, J. W. Bleakley. In the year that Eliza is recorded as working

[41] M. E. McGuire, 'The Legend of the Good Fella Missus' (1990) 14(1/2) *Aboriginal History*, 124.

[42] Ibid., 134.

[43] Liz Conor, *Skin Deep: Settler Impressions of Aboriginal Women* (UWA Press, 2016), 263.

[44] Ibid., 264, quoting Mrs Aeneas Gunn, *The Little Black Princess* (Angus and Robertson, 1905), 175.

[45] Huggins (n 36), 188–189.

for Mrs Steele, he lamented that Aboriginal women were often required to perform arduous tasks without adequate clothing, and were 'almost invariably receiving wages far below the value of their services'.[46]

In common with other Aboriginal people who were subject to the Act, a significant portion of Eliza's wages would have been paid directly to a protector for deposit into a trust account, and the remainder received by her as 'pocket money'. Eliza's ability to make use of the funds in her trust account would have hinged upon the protector's permission:

> The diversion of large proportions of wages into trust accounts meant that Aborigines working under agreements had to seek their Protector's permission to withdraw money for anything other than the very small purchases they could make from their pocket money. Even buying a new skirt or dress, or a minor luxury like a hurricane lamp, required his agreement. The Chief Protector even laid down the type of purchases which could be made at Christmas. The approved purchases included 'cakes, fireworks, dresses, dripping, balloons and whistles but no games with dice ...'[47] (footnotes omitted)

Eliza's thoughts concerning the state's encroachment upon her ability to manage money that she alone had earned are unknown. However, we do know that her life was about to change. For the second time, Eliza would be married.[48]

Marriage

At forty-five years of age, Joe Andrews was fifteen years older than Eliza. Born in Batavia, Joe now lived in Woree where he worked as a 'firewood getter'.[49] It is unknown if the laws and customs of his homeland impacted upon Joe's decision to marry, or how he even viewed the marriage. For

[46] J. W. Bleakley, *Annual Report of the Chief Protector of Aboriginals for the Year 1913* (Anthony James Cumming, Government Printer, 1914), 5.

[47] Robert Castle and Jim Hagan, 'Regulation of Aboriginal Labour in Queensland: Protectors, Agreements and Trust Accounts 1897–1965' (1997) 72 *Labour History*, 66, 69.

[48] Queensland Marriage Certificate, Registration Number 1913/522 2055. The Marriage Certificate provided that Eliza was a widow at the time that she married Joe Andrews.

[49] Ibid.

Eliza, however, it is possible that her approach would have been influenced by memories of the Aboriginal women of her childhood, and laws that had been practiced by countless generations of her family.

One of the tropes of settler representations of Aboriginal women was that of 'bride capture'.[50] From the moment of their 'courtship with a club', Aboriginal wives were portrayed as the victims of their brutish Aboriginal husbands who forced them into lives of drudgery.[51] In reality however, Aboriginal women often enjoyed a degree of equality with Aboriginal men. Historically, Aboriginal women had been the main suppliers of food and healthcare for their communities.[52] They were also keepers of sacred knowledge and ceremony.

Together with Aboriginal men, women participated in the enforcement of marriage laws which were 'proper, orderly, and far more sophisticated' than those of the settlers.[53] Complex systems of kinship classification determined whom one could and could not marry, and such rules were sacrosanct. In Aboriginal societies marriage served multiple purposes, including the brokering of diplomatic ties and cementing access to resources and trade routes. As a consequence, marital contracts were often preceded by long negotiations that involved the relatives of both parties.[54]

Time honoured Aboriginal marriage laws were of little consequence to Queensland's protectionist legislation. Section 9 of the *Aboriginals Protection and Restriction of the Sale of Opium Act 1901* (Qld) provided that:

> No marriage of a female aboriginal with any person other than an aboriginal shall be celebrated without the permission, in writing, of a Protector authorised by the Minister to give such permission.
>
> And the Protector who grants such permission shall forthwith transmit a copy of the same to the Minister.

[50] Conor (n 43), 94.

[51] Ibid.

[52] Sharon Payne, 'Aboriginal Women and the Criminal Justice System' (1990) 2(46) *Aboriginal Law Bulletin*, 9.

[53] Ann McGrath, *Illicit Love: Interracial Sex and Marriage in the United States and Australia* (University of Nebraska Press, 2015), 294.

[54] Ibid., 300.

In respect of marriages to non-Aboriginal men, the Act removed the pivotal role that had been played by families in negotiating the terms of the marital contract. That power was shifted to a hierarchy of public servants, which began with local police officers. In a letter addressed to the Inspector of Police Cairns, one Constable Sticklen of Hambleton advised that he had interviewed 'Joe Andrew the Malay' and 'Eliza the Aboriginal Gin'.[55] He had also made inquiries as to their personal qualities, and determined that both were of good character. The report was subsequently forwarded to the Office of the Chief Protector of Aboriginals in Brisbane.[56] On 16 July the Deputy Chief Protector replied, enclosing a permit authorising the marriage.[57]

Today, it is unsettling to read the words 'Eliza the Aboriginal Gin'. Derived from the Dharug word for woman or wife,[58] the term 'Gin' belonged to a vernacular that dehumanised Aboriginal women. Such language was aligned with print representations that ranged from licentious sirens to domestic servants with grotesque feet and ape-like faces.[59] This system of ideas reduced Aboriginal women to a mere frontier resource.[60] As commodities they were raped, tortured and murdered with impunity.

The horrific violence endured by Aboriginal women was acknowledged by some of the state's Aboriginal 'experts'. In an 1896 report to the Queensland Parliament, one of the architects of the protectionist legislation, Archibald Meston called for 'stringent legislation' to bring an end to

[55] Letter from Constable Sticklen to the Inspector of Police Cairns, 28 June 1913, Queensland State Archives, Eliza and Joe Andrews—Marriages, 1913/1345, Item ID 336450.

[56] Letter from the District Inspector's Office Cairns to the Chief Protector of Aboriginals, 4 July 1913, Queensland State Archives, Eliza and Joe Andrews—Marriages, 1913/1345, Item ID 336450.

[57] Memo from the Deputy Chief Protector of Aboriginals to the Protector of Aboriginals, Cairns, 16 July 1913, Queensland State Archives, Eliza and Joe Andrews—Marriages, 1913/1345, Item ID 336450.

[58] Katelyn Barney, '"We're Women We Fight for Freedom": Intersections of Race and Gender in Contemporary Songs by Indigenous Australian Women Performers' (2008) 22(1) *Women's Studies Journal*, 3, 12.

[59] Conor (n 43).

[60] Ibid., 288.

the abuse of Aboriginal women and children.[61] In apparent frustration, he asked what, 'would the fathers, husbands, and brothers of Queensland do under [similar] circumstances?'[62] Instead of punishing the perpetrators, however, parliamentarians focused on the victims, who became ensnared in the various tentacles of the protectionist regime.

The need to protect Aboriginal women from sexual violence and exploitation was but one of several factors that led to the regulation of marriages between Aboriginal women and non-Aboriginal men. A more influential driver behind s. 9 was the imagined threat posed to European hegemony by unions between Aboriginal women and Asian men.[63] A close reading of the parliamentary debates concerning the passage of the *Aboriginals Protection and Restriction of the Sale of Opium Act 1901* (Qld), reveals that s. 9 was intended to prevent such marriages.

In justifying the provision, the Home Secretary drew upon base stereotypes that painted Asian men as inherently evil and promiscuous:

> The reason why legislation is asked for is that an Asiatic, who is known to have been convicted of offences against the Act – for supplying blacks with opium, for instance – upon a prosecution being attempted against him for a breach of the Act with regard to harbouring a gin and her family, perhaps portion of that family being his own children, does this: He goes through a form of marriage with that gin, and defies the law. There are many such instances. He is a nomad, and that marriage bond is no more to him than a snap of the finger. If he wants to sever it he packs up his traps and goes elsewhere. But he is able, by going through that form of marriage, to defy the protector, and say, "You cannot remove this woman from my premises; she is my wife".[64]

The Home Secretary's opposition to marriages between Aboriginal women and Asian men was shared by those within the state's Indigenous affairs bureaucracy. The Chief Protector for Northern Queensland, Walter Roth was scornful of marriages between Aboriginal women and

[61] Archibald Meston, *Report on the Aboriginals of Queensland* (Government Printer, 1896), 4.

[62] Ibid.

[63] Regina Ganter, 'Living an Immoral Life—"Coloured" Women and the Paternalistic State' (1998) 24(1) *Hecate*, 13.

[64] Queensland, *Parliamentary Debates*, Legislative Assembly, 31 July 1901, 223 (Home Secretary).

Asian men. He considered such unions to be promiscuous even when a church wedding had taken place.[65] Queensland's Chief Protector of Aboriginals, J. W. Bleakley was also strongly opposed to all inter-racial unions.[66]

Therefore, it is surprising that the marriage of Eliza and Joe received an official sanction. Eliza may have wed out of love, pragmatism, or a combination of both. But in marrying a man who was not Aboriginal, Eliza gained a significant advantage. Namely, she became immune to the Minister's power to remove Aboriginal people to Reserves.[67] Two months later, Eliza was working for Isaac Rigg.

Legal Existence

What *The Northern Herald* described as a 'most peculiar case',[68] began in the home of Isaac Rigg in the Cairns suburb of White Rock. During the afternoon of 9 December 1913, Rigg was confronted by one Constable Dempsey. The latter would tell the Cairns Police Court that he had seen Eliza in Riggs' home that day, and that she had been ironing clothes.[69] Dempsey claimed that Eliza told him that she was employed by Rigg without a permit. Later that day Dempsey had a conversation with Joe Andrews, during which the latter produced a certificate of marriage.[70] Riggs was subsequently charged with the offence of unlawfully employing an Aboriginal under s. 14 of the *Aboriginals Protection and Restriction of the Sale of Opium Act 1897* (Qld).

In the Cairns Police Court Rigg's legal representative, Mr MacDonnell claimed that the person formerly known as Eliza Woree had ceased to exist when she married Joe Andrews.[71] Parts of the exchange between

[65] Regina Ganter, *Mixed Relations: Narratives of Asian-Aboriginal Contact in North Australia* (University of Western Australia Press, 2005), 78.

[66] Ibid.

[67] *Aboriginals Protection and Restriction of the Sale of Opium Act 1897* (Qld) s. 10(c).

[68] 'Employing an Aboriginal. The Lubra Who Was Married. What Control Has the Protector? Is the Wedding Ceremony All a Farce' *The Northern Herald* (Cairns) (26 December 1913), 26, https://trove.nla.gov.au/newspaper/rendition/nla.news-article147173600.3.pdf?followup=e536e071b1158fc97356e1ba64184b01.

[69] Ibid.

[70] Ibid.

[71] Ibid.

Mr MacDonnell and the Police Magistrate (The PM), Mr P. G. Grant, were reported by the *Northern Herald*:

> Mr MacDonnell said his defence was that there was no such person as Eliza Woree now. Some time ago she was married to a Malay.
> The P.M.: When a woman is married she takes the nationality of her husband.
> Mr MacDonnell: That is my contention.
> The P.M.: She ceases to be an aboriginal so far as the law is concerned.
> Mr MacDonnell: That being so, it is no offence to employ her. I admit she was on the premises of Mr Rigg.
> The P.M.: Why shouldn't she be? Did her husband know where she was?
> Mr MacDonnell: Yes. She works for Mr. Rigg in the day and goes home to her husband at night.[72]

Eliza already suffered an inferior status as a result of both the racial hierarchy that was enmeshed in northern Queensland, and the invasive provisions of the protectionist legislation. Now, she had become all but invisible under the common law. Under the principle of coverture, a woman lost her legal identity upon marriage. The rationale of coverture was articulated by William Blackstone in the eighteenth century:

> By marriage, the husband and wife are one person in law: that is, the very being or legal existence of the woman is suspended during the marriage, or at least is incorporated and consolidated into that of the husband; under whose wing, protection and *cover*, she performs every thing; and is therefore called in our law-french a *feme covert* ... under the protection and influence of her husband, her *baron* or lord; and her condition during her marriage is called her *coverture*.[73]

As she was without a legal identity, a married woman could not hold property, enter into contracts or manage her own wages.[74] This loss of autonomy extended to physical inviolability. Husbands were entitled to

[72] Ibid.

[73] Claudia Zaher, 'When a Woman's Marital Status Determined Her Legal Status: A Research Guide on the Common Law Doctrine of Coverture' (2002) 94(3) *Law Library Journal*, 459, 460.

[74] Linda J. Kirk, 'Exclusion to Emancipation: A Comparative Analysis of Women's Citizenship in Australia and the United States 1861–1921' (1995) 97(3) *West Virginia Law Review*, 725, 727.

subject wives to 'moderate correction' in the form of physical punishment,[75] and rape was considered merely a form of trespass rather than a horrific act of violence.[76] It followed that marital rape was an impossibility, because a husband could not commit a trespass in respect of an object over which he held proprietary rights.[77]

Coverture began to unravel in the closing decades of the nineteenth century when married women gained the ability to divorce and the right to hold property.[78] Just as married women were gaining property rights, however, they became subject to the international phenomenon of marital denaturalisation.[79] Whereas a husband's allegiance was owed to his country, a wife's allegiance was owed to her husband. It followed that by marrying an 'alien' a woman lost her nationality and, at least in theory, gained that of her husband.[80]

According to the logic of coverture, Eliza lost her legal existence upon marrying Joe. Her identity merged into his. Furthermore, Eliza had also lost her Australian nationality. It is unlikely, however, that Eliza had previously been aware of this change to her status. Given that Eliza was present at the hearing in the Cairns Police Court,[81] one can only imagine what she thought of such discussions.

The prosecutor, Sergeant Hawkes countered that the marriage had resulted only in Eliza becoming exempt from one provision of the *Aboriginals Protection and Restriction of the Sale of Opium Acts 1897–1901* (Qld), which the Magistrate inferred to be the Minister's removals power

[75] Henry Finlay, 'Lawmaking in the Shadow of the Empire: Divorce in Colonial Australia' (1999) 24(1) *Journal of Family History*, 74, 75.

[76] Alecia Simmonds, 'Courtship, Coverture and Marital Cruelty: Historicising Intimate Violence in the Civil Courts' (2019) 45(1) *Australian Feminist Law Journal*, 131, 139.

[77] Ibid.

[78] Ibid., 140.

[79] British Nationality and Status of Aliens Act, 1914, 4 & 5 Geo. V, c. 17, s. 10(1). See M. Page Baldwin, 'Subject to Empire: Married Women and the British Nationality and Status of Aliens Act' (2001) 40(4) *The Journal of British Studies*, 522.

[80] Helen Irving, *Citizenship, Alienage, and the Modern Constitutional State: A Gendered History* (Cambridge University Press, 2016), 73–74.

[81] *Dempsey v Rigg* [1914] St R Qd 245. According to the headnote, Eliza and Joe were 'personally produced at the hearing of the prosecution' where they were 'identified in cross-examination by Constable Dempsey'.

in s. 9.[82] Sergeant Hawkes also produced a succinct wire from the Crown Law Office in support of his submission.[83] The implication that Eliza remained subject to the remaining provisions of the Act sparked the following exchange:

> The P.M.: Can you interfere with her after she is legally married? If so, then what is the use of her getting married?
> Mr MacDonnell: She could not live with her husband according to that. Following the same line of argument, if she does live with her husband, then he is liable for every day that she is there. He could be prosecuted for harbouring her. The whole thing is simply nonsense.
> The P.M.: It is against all my ideas of common sense that after a woman is legally married she should not be under the control of her husband.
> Mr MacDonnell: They cannot shift her to a reserve, and if she is not to live with him what is she to do. How absurd.
> The P.M.: According to the marriage certificate she was married with the consent of everyone concerned.
> Mr MacDonnell: What is the object of the consent if this sort of thing is to go on?
> Mr P.M.: I ask, too, what is the use of her getting married?
> Mr MacDonnell: She cannot live with her husband if Sergeant Hawkes's contention is correct.
> The P.M.: I cannot see how I can go against my conception of common law and common sense. I don't see how I can convict defendant for employing an aboriginal. I take it that this woman is subject to the control of her husband and nobody else. It is a perfect farce going through the marriage ceremony if the husband is not to have control.
> Sergeant Hawkes: The Crown Law Office evidently thinks different.
> The P.M.: They might be right or they might not. Perhaps the Chief Protector of Aboriginals (Mr Howard) can give us some information on the point. My view is that it is a wonderful thing if a lawfully married husband cannot have the sole control of his wife.[84]

[82] 'Employing an Aboriginal. The Lubra Who Was Married. What Control Has the Protector? Is the Wedding Ceremony All a Farce' *The Northern Herald* (Cairns) (26 December 1913), 26, https://trove.nla.gov.au/newspaper/rendition/nla.news-article147173600.3.pdf?followup=e536e071b1158fc97356e1ba64184b01.

[83] Ibid.

[84] Ibid.

Magistrate Grant dismissed the complaint. He also stated a special case under s. 227 of the *Justices Act 1886* (Qld)[85]; a procedure in which a question of law is submitted to another court for its determination. The question of law submitted to the Northern Supreme Court was:

> … whether Eliza Woree, an aboriginal, having been married to one Joe Andrews, a Malay, according to law, and with the consent of the Chief Protector of Aboriginals, was still subject to the provisions of *The Aboriginals Protection and Restriction of the Sale of Opium Acts*, 1897 to 1901.[86]

Justice Jameson answered the question in the affirmative and remitted the matter back to the Police Magistrate.[87] Isaac Rigg appealed to the Full Court of the Supreme Court of Queensland. His counsel, A. D. Graham, once again argued that upon marrying Joe Andrews, Eliza had ceased to be an Aboriginal for the purposes of the Act. She had 'passed from the protection of the State under the Aboriginals Acts to the protection of her husband under the general law'.[88]

He also appealed to the potential inconvenience that could be suffered by the husbands of Aboriginal women who continued to be regulated by the Act:

> Mr Graham submitted that in the eyes of the law the woman had ceased to be an aboriginal on her marriage with a Dutchman. Further, if an aboriginal woman or half caste woman was not exempted from the Act any man who married her would be liable to punishment for keeping her on his premises, or moving her out of the district in which she married. There were many white men and Chinamen married to aboriginal women or half-caste women, and if the complainant's contention were right, they would be in a very peculiar position. It might be questioned whether an aboriginal could keep his gin without the consent of the protector.[89]

[85] *Dempsey v Rigg* [1914] St R Qd 245.

[86] Ibid., 246.

[87] Ibid.

[88] Ibid., 247.

[89] 'Supreme Court: Full Court Sittings' *Telegraph* (Brisbane, 5 June 1914) 2, http://nla.gov.au/nla.news-article176167642.

The respondent's counsel, Mr E. Hobbs countered that the appellant had failed to distinguish between race and nationality. The Act was concerned only with race, and the nationality of those who were regulated under the Act was of no consequence.[90] The Full Court agreed. In the lead judgment, Cooper CJ wrote that Eliza's marriage 'did not make her anything different from an aboriginal'.[91] As Isaac Rigg did not have a protector's permission to employ Eliza, he had committed an offence under s. 14 of the Act.

Real, Chubb and Lukin JJ concurred. According to Chubb J, the case was about race rather than nationality, and a 'man or woman [could] no more change their race than a leopard can change its spots'.[92] The matter was sent back to the Cairns Summons Court, where Isaac Rigg was subsequently sentenced to a fine of 6d, and in default, a minute's imprisonment.[93]

The decision was instructive of how the protectionist legislation operated in conjunction with the common law to render Aboriginal women invisible. The issues raised by the case were of crucial significance to Eliza, impinging upon both her freedom and her nationality. Yet she was utterly voiceless. Eliza would have surely known that her opinions and aspirations were irrelevant to the men who wielded so much power over her life. But like other Aboriginal outlaw women, Eliza was resourceful and she would use her wits to empower herself.

Part Three: Deportation to Palm Island

Life in Malay Town

Six years after the Full Court handed down its decision in *Dempsey v Rigg*, Eliza once again came under the scrutiny of the authorities. By then the marriage between Eliza and Joe had broken down, and the two had not

[90] Ibid.

[91] *Dempsey v Rigg* [1914] St R Qd 254, 248.

[92] Ibid.

[93] 'A "Sprat" Fine' *Balonne Beacon* (St George, 2 July 1914), 2, https://trove.nla.gov.au/newspaper/article/215380992?searchTerm=Isaac%20and%20Rigg%20and%20Cairns&searchLimits=.

cohabited for 'some considerable time'.[94] Eliza was now living in Upper Kenny Street in Cairns, which fell within the informal settlement known as 'Malaytown'. The settlement had been built on the banks of Alligator Creek in the 1880s by Malaysian labourers who aspired to create a place where they belonged.[95] Malaytown soon became a diverse community that included Torres Strait Islanders, Javanese, Japanese, Chinese, Filipinos, Pacific Islanders and Aboriginal people.[96]

Malaytown first sparked media attention in 1904 as a consequence of a fatal case of bubonic plague. The *Cairns Morning Post* reported that the body of one Honssain, a Singhalese cook was found in Malaytown on 12 March.[97] Upon confirming the cause of death the Government Medical Officer, Dr. Cumming proceeded to Malaytown accompanied by police officers. After residents were given a brief opportunity to remove their belongings from their homes, the dwellings were doused with kerosene and set alight.[98] The residents of Malaytown were obviously resilient, because they soon returned. Their renewed presence was followed by the establishment of a police station nearby. Out of deference to the sensitivities of local Europeans, the station was called 'South Cairns' rather than Malaytown.[99]

What little has been written about Malaytown reveals that it was a lively place. Former residents who lived in Malaytown as children in the 1930s have reflected on a vibrant community, renowned for its Saturday night dances and feasts.[100] It has also been described as an open and generous

[94] Letter from Constable E. M. James to the Protector of Aboriginals Cairns, 21 September 1921, Queensland State Archives, Eliza—Trust Accounts—Transfer and Miscellaneous, 1922.1010, Item ID 336727.

[95] Woods (n 33), 125.

[96] Chatenay cited by Lisa Law, 'The Ghosts of White Australia: Excavating the Past(s) of Rusty's Market in Tropical Cairns' (2011) 25(5) *Continuum: Journal of Media and Cultural Studies*, 669, 675.

[97] 'The Plague' *Cairns Morning Post* (Cairns, 15 March 1904), 5, https://trove.nla.gov.au/newspaper/rendition/nla.news-article42957623.txt.

[98] Ibid.

[99] Jeremy Hodes, 'Malaytown Talk pt. 2', *Queensland History* (Blogpost, 8 March 2011) http://queenslandhistory.blogspot.com/2011/03/malaytown-talk-pt-2.html.

[100] 'Malaytown,' *Earshot* (Miyuki Jokiranta, ABC Radio National, 15 September 2015), https://www.abc.net.au/radionational/programs/earshot/malaytown/6746408.

neighbourhood.[101] Some of the magic of Malaytown captured the imagination of a small number of prominent artists and writers in the 1930s. The writer, Jean Devanny established close friendships with prominent Torres Strait Islander families such as the Pitts and the Sailors.[102] The artist, Ian Fairweather also had a sojourn in Malaytown; an experience that inspired paintings such as *Alligator Creek*.

The residents of Malaytown enjoyed relative autonomy and with few exceptions, the Aboriginal people who lived there managed their own wages.[103] For possibly the first time in her life, Eliza was able to make choices concerning her employment and the expenditure of any money that she earned. I would like to think that Eliza became a patron of Malaytown's famous Saturday evening dances, where guests swayed to live music.[104]

Due to the makeshift nature of Malaytown and its position on the 'swampy side of town',[105] Eliza's new life would have involved a degree of hardship. I imagine that, like other residents, she dwelt in a makeshift shack positioned on stilts.[106] When the tide was in some homes would flood with water, forcing the occupants to leave and wait until the tide had receded.[107] According to Hodes, malaria was also 'rife' and ablution facilities were basic, with only one shower in the entire settlement.[108] Nonetheless, Eliza was independent, being answerable to neither a husband nor a protector. Tragically, her freedom was only temporary.

The Loss of Freedom

Eliza's journey back to subjugation was sparked by the suspicion that she was operating as a prostitute. In a brief memorandum dated 16

[101] Ibid.

[102] Carole Ferrier, 'Jean Devanny: Romantic Revolutionary' (1997) 21(54–55) *Journal of Australian Studies*, 30, 34.

[103] Ganter (n 65), 200.

[104] Miyuki Jokiranta (n 100).

[105] Ganter (n 65), 200.

[106] Hodes (n 99).

[107] Miyuki Jokiranta, (n 100).

[108] Ibid.

September 1921, Constable E. M. James of Cairns Station made the following allegations:

> I beg to report that [Eliza Woree] has for some considerable time past resided at Upper Kenny Street, Cairns. That portion of the Town is better known as Malaytown where a large number of Malays and others reside. I have received very reliable information from different sources that Eliza is carrying on as a Prostitute, and that she is visited regularly by Japanese, Malays, Aboriginals and others. Several complaints have been made to me of late regarding the conduct of this Gin. This Gin as far as I can ascertain is very much against signing on to any employee, and she certainly has a very great influence [over] other Aboriginals living in this locality. I would recommend that she be removed to Palm Island Mission Station.[109]

I can imagine the sweat on the Constable's brow as he bristled at this Aboriginal woman who had clearly become too opinionated for his liking. The Constable's anger may have also been fuelled by double standards. The exploitation of Aboriginal women by white men was often dismissed as a necessary evil in frontier towns in which white women were few.[110] In contrast, sexual unions between Aboriginal women and Asian men were vilified as a threat to the public good. Women who engaged in such liaisons were assumed to be prostitutes,[111] and their male partners were pilloried for depriving white men of what they considered to be their exclusive resource.

Not only had Eliza apparently committed the sin of engaging in sex with Asian men. She had also refused to sign on to an employment agreement and become one of the state's many disenfranchised Aboriginal workers. To make matters worse, Eliza was asserting a 'very great influence' over other Aboriginal people. In other words, she was an intelligent and outspoken woman who had exercised considerable ingenuity in evading the Office of the Chief Protector of Aboriginals for sometime.

Now that she had returned to the attention of the authorities, Eliza was vulnerable to deportation to a Reserve. Section 9 of the *Aboriginals*

[109] Letter from Constable E. M. James to the Protector of Aboriginals Cairns, 16 September 1921, Queensland State Archives, Eliza—Trust Accounts—Transfer and Miscellaneous, 1922.1010, Item ID 336727.

[110] Conor (n 43), 324.

[111] Ibid., 290.

Protection and Restriction of the Sale of Opium Act 1897 (Qld) provided that:

> It shall be lawful for the Minister to cause every aboriginal within any District, not being an aboriginal excepted from the provisions of this section, to be removed to, and kept within the limits of, any reserve situated within such District, in such manner, and subject to such conditions, as may be prescribed. The Minister may, subject to the said conditions, cause any aboriginal to be removed from one reserve to another.

The Minister's power of removal fulfilled a number of purposes. It allowed for the extraction of the sick and the elderly from fringe camps to institutions. Aboriginal people who were suspected of committing criminal offences could be deported to reserves in lieu of a trial.[112] Removals also maintained European hegemony. Aboriginal people who had the temerity to question their subjugation were deported to Reserves to be punished.

Section 10 provided exceptions to the exercise of the Minister's power in s. 9. Those who were lawfully employed,[113] held a permit to be absent from a Reserve,[114] or were able to persuade the Minister that 'satisfactory provision' had been made for their welfare,[115] were beyond the ambit of s. 9. Likewise, an Aboriginal woman who was lawfully married to and residing with a husband who was not Aboriginal was excluded.[116] Unable to avail herself of any of the exceptions in s.10, Eliza's fate was sealed. She would become one of the almost 7000 people who were removed to Reserves between the passage of the *Aboriginals Protection and Restriction of the Sale of Opium Act* in 1897 and its repeal in 1939.[117]

On 9 October 1921, the Home Secretary, William McCormack signed an order for Eliza's removal to the Palm Island Reserve.[118] Under the

[112] Thom Blake, 'Deported … At the Sweet Will of the Government: The Removal of Aborigines to Reserves in Queensland 1897–1939' (1998) 22 *Aboriginal History*, 51, 57.

[113] *Aboriginals Protection and Restriction of the Sale of Opium Act 1897* (Qld) s. 10(a).

[114] Ibid., s. 10(b).

[115] Ibid., s. 10(d).

[116] Ibid., s. 10(c).

[117] Blake (n 112).

[118] Order for Removal of Aboriginals, 9 October 1921, Queensland State Archives, Eliza—Trust Accounts—Transfer and Miscellaneous, 1922.1010, Item ID 3367/27.

section titled 'offence and cause for removal' was a single word—'prostitute'.[119] There would be no hearing during which the allegations against Eliza could be tested. Likewise, she had no means of appealing against the Home Secretary's decision. On 10 October 1921, the Office of the Chief Protector of Aboriginals forwarded the order for Eliza's removal to the Commissioner of Police.[120] On 16 November Eliza was arrested at the Cairns Watch House,[121] where she presumably spent the night. The following morning, Eliza boarded the S. S. Kuranda for the voyage to Palm Island.[122] I can imagine that she was hurt, shocked and angry. The fear of being incarcerated far away from everything and everyone that she had ever known, would have been palpable.

Home to the Manbarra people and Bwgcolman people, Palm Island is 213 kilometres south of Cairns. In 1914 it was gazetted as a Reserve as part of J. W. Bleakley's drive to quarantine Aboriginal wards, who would have to contend with shark-infested waters if they were desirous of escape.[123] Palm Island would become the place where 'troublesome cases'[124] such as Eliza were sent to be disciplined. For most of her incarceration, Palm Island was under the tumultuous and despotic rule of Superintendent Robert Henry Curry.

Curry was notorious for his strict enforcement of racial segregation. Homes that inmates had constructed with their bare hands were used to house white officials, and the surrounds declared 'out of bounds' to Aboriginal people.[125] As distinct from the white staff who received superior food and were waited on by domestic servants,[126] inmates led

[119] Ibid.

[120] Letter from the Chief Protector of Aboriginals to the Commissioner of Police, 10 October 1921, Queensland State Archives, Eliza—Trust Accounts—Transfer and Miscellaneous, 1922.1010, Item ID 336727.

[121] Letter from Acting Sergeant H. S. Martin to Inspector Daley, Cairns, 19 November 1921, Queensland State Archives, Eliza—Trust Accounts—Transfer and Miscellaneous, 1922.1010, Item ID 336727.

[122] Ibid.

[123] Joanne Watson, *Palm Island Through a Long Lens* (Aboriginal Studies Press, 2010), 32.

[124] Toby Martin, '"Socialist Paradise" or "Inhospitable Island"? Visitor Responses to Palm Island in the 1920s and 1930s' (2014) 38 *Aboriginal History*, 131, 133.

[125] Watson (n 123), 40.

[126] Ibid., 85.

wretched lives. Each morning began with a roll call before they were sent to work in the various roles that were crucial to the functioning of the Reserve; such as building roads, clearing land for farming, carpentry, cleaning and baking.[127]

As an inmate, Eliza would have been compelled to provide a minimum of 24 hours of unpaid labour per week.[128] When her day came to an end, I imagine that Eliza slept in a dormitory together with other women who were under the supervision of the 'dormitory boss'.[129] Those who attempted to abscond often suffered inhumane punishments that included having their heads shaved.[130] Inmates were expected to survive on woefully inadequate rations,[131] with deleterious impacts on their health. By Eliza's third year on Palm Island, the death rate had spiralled to more than 16%.[132]

Given such terrible conditions, it is surprising that Palm Island was a popular tourist attraction during the time of Eliza's incarceration. Tourists were drawn to the Island in order to come face to face with 'primitive peoples',[133] who were apparently living in a 'socialist' paradise.[134] Given her outspokenness and independent spirit I imagine that Eliza resented the prying visitors, who were oblivious to the various degradations suffered by inmates.

Both Curry's reign and his life ended brutally in an insane rampage. On the evening of 2 February 1930, Curry murdered his son and step-daughter before wounding the settlement doctor and his wife.[135] Curry set several buildings alight and then retreated in a boat. While departmental staff hid with their families in the bush,[136] Aboriginal people were

[127] Ibid., 42.

[128] Ibid., 39.

[129] Joanne Watson, 'A Century of Activism and Heartache: The Troubled History of Palm Island' (2018) 60 *Griffith Review*, https://test.griffithreview.com/editions/first-things-first/.

[130] Ibid.

[131] Watson (n 123), 39.

[132] Ibid.

[133] Martin (n 124), 136.

[134] Ibid., 135.

[135] Watson (n 123), 55–56.

[136] Ibid., 60.

left to defend the settlement. The siege lasted for sixteen hours, ending only when Curry was shot and killed by an inmate, Peter Prior, who was acting on the orders of officials.[137]

From what is known about Eliza's story she emerges as a brave and strong-willed woman. So it is unsurprising that Eliza's spirit was not broken by the injustice of her incarceration. In 1932 she took what was perhaps a final leap of faith, and agreed to marry a fellow inmate, Joe Salmon. Permission to marry was duly granted. However, the marriage never proceeded because Eliza remained married to Joe Andrews.[138] Three years later, Eliza died on Palm Island.[139] My late father often spoke about what happens to us in death. According to Dad, we return to our old people. If he was right, then Eliza left the final vestige of her incarceration and was wrapped in the embrace of her loved ones.

Conclusion

Eliza Woree is a name that all Australians should know. In a better world, she would be synonymous with qualities such as fortitude and ingenuity. She escaped death on a brutal frontier and unlike so many other survivors of the invasion, Eliza did not succumb to starvation or the numerous diseases that flow from abject poverty and official neglect. Somehow, this outlaw woman found a way to survive in a world that treated Black women with callous indifference at best.

By imagining the junctures of her brief life, we are reminded that Aboriginal women's experiences of colonisation have been defined by unrelenting violence, from which the law has rarely offered a haven. Eliza's story also serves as a litmus test; making visible the influences of racism and patriarchy upon the law. The protectionist legislation and the common law were a lethal combination for Aboriginal women such as Eliza. The former stripped Eliza of autonomy in aspects of her life such as marriage and employment, before cruelly subjecting her to indefinite incarceration. The latter denied her a legal existence upon entering into marriage.

[137] Ibid., 61–62.

[138] Letter from Ernest Gribble to the Chief Protector, 10 December 1932, Queensland State Archives, Eliza Andrews and Joe Salmon—Marriages, 1932/8573, Item ID 336474.

[139] Eliza Andrews—Death Register, 1935, p. 55, Queensland State Archives, Item ID 302716.

But like other outlaw women, Eliza never succumbed to her oppression. Each step in her journey is a lesson about the indomitability of the human spirit. Eliza and her sisters call out from the forgotten pages of history. If we close our eyes and open our hearts, then perhaps we will have the great fortune of hearing them.

CHAPTER 5

Conclusion

Abstract This chapter provides a succinct summary of the themes raised in the substantive chapters. It describes the tenets of outlaw culture, and names some of the women who were at the vanguard of this body of empowering practices. It concludes by arguing that the stories of Black outlaw women are important. It is through the telling of such stories that Indigenous people can begin to heal from the injustices of the past, and Australian society can come to value the contributions made by Black outlaw women.

Keywords Conclusion · Indigenous women · Importance of hearing our voices

In common with chapter one, this concluding chapter will share some of my own stories. When I commenced my journey in the Academy two decades ago, I belonged to the first generation of Indigenous scholars to be employed in Australia's law schools. I began my role as a junior academic with optimism about my capacity to make a difference. Naively, I believed that because the glass ceiling had been broken, Indigenous people's stories and experiential knowledge of the law would finally be recognised, and perhaps, even appreciated by legal scholars. I quickly

N. Watson, *Aboriginal Women, Law and Critical Race Theory*, Palgrave Studies in Race, Ethnicity, Indigeneity and Criminal Justice, https://doi.org/10.1007/978-3-030-87327-1_5

realised, however, that law schools are complex institutions that are resistant to change.

It was not until I stumbled upon critical race theory ('CRT') that I could finally see my own reflection in academic scholarship. Although our cultures and histories were not the same, I could relate to the stories described by American CRT scholars, who had also been similarly wounded by their experiences of law schools. As someone who grew up in a family that valued oral storytelling, I was moved by articles that cast light on the narratives of outsiders. I was also inspired by the words of critical race feminists ('CRF'), who brought the lived experience of women of colour to the centre of their scholarship. Finally, the work of CRF scholars on women outlaws resonated with the matriarchs who have played, and continue to play, an important role in my own life. Sadly, however, Indigenous women have rarely been valued in Australian society.

Australia has a violent and tragic relationship with Black women. From the beginning of colonisation, Indigenous women were represented through various tropes, such as bride capture, the jezebel, and even the barbarous mother who practiced cannibalism on her own children. Those tropes obscured unpalatable truths about the founding of Australia, and deflected from the violence unleashed by colonisation. Colonial myths also obscured the reality that Indigenous women have rarely enjoyed the protection of the law.

The stories of the Black women that appeared in the pages of this book provide a glimpse of the horrors endured by generations. Kowaha felt compelled to throw herself and her infant daughter from the summit of Mount Mandurana, rather than suffer at the hands of the Native Police. The teenage servant, Maggie was viciously attacked by her employer, who callously allowed her to suffer on the floor of his fowl house.

The failure of the law to protect Indigenous women spurred the development of a body of practices, values and tactics to create spaces of safety. Indigenous women's outlaw culture manifests in a gamut of relationships with the law. At one end of the spectrum are women who found safety through breaking the law. Tarenorerer broke free from a life of brutal servitude, and engaged in armed combat against the invaders. Mary Ann Bugg embraced the life of a bushranger during her years as the partner and accomplice of Captain Thunderbolt. Other outlaw women fled from oppressive institutions that were created in order to implement the protection and assimilation policies. Some risked their liberty to take strike action in the pursuit of a fair wage.

Transgressing the law is but one aspect of outlaw culture. Another is operating within the boundaries of the law to create spaces of safety for the most disadvantaged members of one's community. For some women, this meant providing love and care for vulnerable children. Others were among the founders of community-controlled organisations that deliver crucial services in the fields of health, law and child care. Indigenous women's outlaw culture is yet to attract academic analysis. But examples abound in oral histories, life stories and accounts of ground-breaking actions, such as the 1946 strike by Aboriginal workers in the Pilbara. Another potential source of outlaw stories is legal storytelling.

When Indigenous women appear in the judgments of Australian courts, their stories are often missing. In cases such as *Tuckiar v R*,[1] which is discussed in chapter three, the Yolngu women were not named. Although at least one of them witnessed the killing of Constable McColl, none were called to give evidence at the subsequent trial. We will never know how the events that took place on the day of McColl's death, or the trial that followed, impacted upon their lives. This absence of Indigenous women's stories is at odds with one aspect of outlaw culture, which is using the law to protect both Country and community. As discussed in chapter three, Indigenous women have used litigation as a means of safeguarding precious relics and the voting rights of prisoners.

This book has argued that the stories of the Indigenous women who linger in the background of judgments can be constructed through the medium of speculative biography. When the traces of their lives that remain on the public record are combined with socio-legal materials, instances of outlaw culture can be gleaned. In chapter four this methodology was used to imagine the life of Eliza Woree, an Aboriginal woman who featured in the factual scenario that provided the background to the decision of the Supreme Court of Queensland in *Dempsey v Rigg* [1914] St R Qd 245.

Isaac Rigg was charged with the offence of unlawfully employing an Aboriginal, in breach of the provisions of the *Aboriginals Protection and Restriction of the Sale of Opium Act 1897* (Qld), when he employed Eliza without first obtaining official sanction. Rigg argued that because Eliza had married a foreigner she had lost her nationality, and therefore, she

[1] *Tuckiar v R* (1934) 52 CLR 335.

was no longer an Aboriginal within the meaning of the Act. His argument was rejected by the Supreme Court of Queensland. Even though she was central to the facts, Eliza's narrative was missing from the judgments. In chapter four, I drew upon archival records, historical accounts and newspaper reports to imagine her life story. Although temporary, Eliza managed to escape the grasp of Queensland's Indigenous affairs bureaucracy and create an independent life for herself.

The stories of the Indigenous women who were at the vanguard of outlaw culture are rich and inspiring. When relegated to the bottom step of the colonial hierarchy, Black women found ingenious means to protect themselves and their loved ones. The narratives of those indomitable women need to be told. Their courage, resourcefulness and foresight have the capacity to move readers from all walks of life. Through telling their stories, we may begin to heal from the grave injustices of the past, and start to see injustices of the present through new lenses. Australians might also begin to value the lives of the outlaw women's descendants, who continue to practice this crucial tradition of keeping their families and communities safe.

The manufacturer's authorised representative in the EU is Springer Nature Customer Service Centre GmbH, Europaplatz 3, 69115 Heidelberg, Germany. If you have any concerns regarding our products, please contact ProductSafety@springernature.com

Printed and bound by CPI Group (UK) Ltd, Croydon, CR0 4YY
30/09/2026
02225260-0001